Burton Printing Company/Comet Publishing/
4270 S. Saginaw St.
Burton, MI 48529
(810) 742-3210
email: burtonprinting@gmail.com

St. Luke N.E.W. Life Center

VOICES

By
Sr. Judy Blake CSJ
with
Sr. Carol Weber OP

TABLE OF CONTENTS

MERCY

COMPASSION

PASSION FOR THE MISSION

DEDICATION

This book is dedicated to the thousands of volunteers who have given of their time, talent, property and money to help the St. Luke N.E.W. Life Center carry out its mission.

God Bless you all.

Foreword by Father Tom

Two Catholic nuns decided to combine their missions and do their corporal and spiritual works of mercy for the benefit of the people in the northend of Flint, Michigan. When St. Luke's parish closed, Bishop Earl Boyea gave the school building and property to Sister Judy and Sister Carol. This was the start of the St. Luke N.E.W. Life Center. From that humble beginning thousands of people have had their lives made better because they became involved with the Center.

My dear friends, money does not cure poverty. Love cures poverty. For anyone who is truly loved is not poor. By helping people gain their self-esteem and realize their worth as a child of God, the St. Luke N.E.W. Life Center has not only made those people's lives better, but it has enriched the lives of everyone they touch. For to be able to love your neighbor, you first must learn to love yourself. That is just what the Center does. It helps people learn to love themselves so they can love their neighbors, and the world is a better place.

This book records the voices of just a few of the people whose lives have been so changed. God Bless everyone involved with the St. Luke N.E.W. Life Center, and may God Bless each person to whom this book comes.

Fr. Tom Firestone

ST. LUKE N.E.W. LIFE CENTER
MISSION STATEMENT

St. Luke N.E.W. Life Center is a faith-based environment providing life skills, education and workplace training, empowering women and men to become self-sufficient.

LIVING THE MISSION

We are committed to building trusting and enduring relationships with the families who receive assistance through our programs. To receive support from N.E.W. Life, an individual must have a genuine desire to change his or her situation and must regularly participate in activities for the duration of the program in which she or he is enrolled. Our programs are for personal growth and development. They include counseling, spiritual and life experience, growth of self-esteem individually and in support groups.

Our employment preparation programs train our women and men for the workforce. They learn how to respond to a supervisor, not just react. They learn how to focus and work hard. In order to test their readiness for employment we started social enterprises: a sewing business, greenhouse gardening and pallet making for the women and lawn care, snow removal, greenhouse gardening and pallet making for the men. They are paid for their on-the-job training and learn a work ethic so they can be employed in the regular work force.

We also operate a food pantry that provides two meals a week and distributes food for more than 100 families each week. We serve over 3,000 people monthly. We also have a variety of community services, including crisis intervention, childcare, eyecare, legal assistance, social service counseling and a Literacy Center which helps people prepare and obtain their GED. These services are critical to the success of our workforce programming, as they provide participants with additional wrap-around services required to support their families as well as real-world experience during the program. Furthermore, our community services help us build trust with people in the community, that ultimately move on to enroll in programs that address generational poverty. Many of the people in our employment preparation programs and social enterprises were introduced to NEW Life through our food pantry or crisis intervention services.

PROLOGUE

Sister Judy

We are bombarded by voices every day. Some are disturbing: the voice of a women who jumped out of a window of her home wearing only her pajamas, carrying only her cell phone, to avoid being beaten, possibly to death. Some voices are joyful: those who generously want to help as a volunteer, drop off a monetary, clothing or other donations and those who bring rescued food from a nearby hospital or restaurant. We know how to respond to those voices--- experience has taught us well. But there are other voices that are puzzling, For instance, the spiritual voices.

Sister Judy

In 1991 I was in my 13th year as a Catholic nun with the Society of St. Joseph when my religious community gifted me with a 30 day retreat. It had a double blessing. It was in Sedalia, Colorado, my favorite state, and part of my family lived in Colorado. I was moving from a suburban parish to a poor city parish in the north end of Flint so I looked forward to this retreat to help me explore, with God's help, how this new ministry would be different and where God was leading me.

While on retreat I had a recurring dream. In my dream I

saw a group of women standing in front of a brick building. **But the women had no faces**. As I approached them, they started pleading for help.

"Help us. Please help us. We are gifted and talented, but we need your help."

I said nothing and walked away. I shared the dream with the director of the Sacred Heart Jesuit Retreat House. She felt that God was trying to communicate a message to me. She advised me to pray for the meaning of this dream. I did. But dream remained the same.

Arriving home I shared with Sister Carol what happened on retreat. Her advice was the same. Keep praying for clarity. I was not sure that I wanted an answer. I put this event on the back burner of my mind. God, however, kept pestering me with the same dream. And one day I had to respond.

Sister Carol Weber OP

The Mission Begins

One Sunday in winter, Sister Carol came home looking like a woman on a mission. She was. She was a sponsor for her niece for confirmation and had to attend class with her once a month. Carol didn't even take off her coat and hang it up. Instead, with her coat still on, she sat on the edge of her chair and looked at me. I said, "What's up?" She asked me when was I ever going to do something about my dream. Three years had passed. I never expected that question. "I don't know, why?" I said. "I think I have an idea for you," Sister Carol said. (She had had an hour between the class and home to think about it.) "So what is it?" I asked. "How about doing a clothes collection for the homeless?" said Sister Carol. "Alison (her niece) will make some scarves and maybe we can make some cookies." I asked her where we could go to find the people to give them to. She said, "I don't know, maybe down by the railroad tracks or maybe the soup kitchen." (Now there has to be hundreds of train tracks around Flint because of the car companies.) So I said, "I think the soup kitchen would work great."

Sister Carol said, "At Mass on Sunday we can ask for warm clothes and the following Saturday we can distribute them." Whoa," I said, "When is this project due?" She replied, "In two weeks." Two weeks? This **was** going to happen. So I asked my confirmation families if they wanted to use this event for their service hours. I got only one family, a mom and two kids.

The Friday evening before, Alison came to our house. She and Aunt Carol baked cookies, peanut butter, because they have protein in them. We had more than enough cookies, but they wouldn't even let me do a taste test. Saturday we had two loaded vans of clothing and the cookies. My confirmation candidate and her mom had come with a van load. We went to the north end of Flint in front of the North End Soup Kitchen and started to hand out clothes from the vans. Without ever having to advertise or say anything, about 10 minutes after we had set up there were 100 people there. It was really cold that day and we shivered as we did so but the homeless and needy were more than glad to see us.

John Manse, the director of the soup kitchen, came out and invited us inside. Some of the men came out to help us bring everything inside. Alison started passing out the scarves and the people began walking around, modeling them. They were very excited about the cookies. One man came up to Sister Carol and asked her, "Do you know these are homemade cookies?" " Yes," she said. "Do you know how long it's been since I had a homemade cookie?" "No", she said. "It's been 41 years." A little tear trickled down his cheek. A tender memory from the past for me.

Well, it was a great experience done and over with. We got back to the church and unloaded the empty boxes. As I was about to thank my parishioner for her help, she said, "Sister Judy, we have to keep doing this. Those people really need us and our help. I am there and my whole family will be there." I asked her to tell the parish what this experience was like and see if they wanted to help. They did. We had just initiated a new ministry for our parishioners.

We started going out monthly on the streets and we grew bigger and bigger. We would take a little lunch. We did hot dogs and chips and Sunny D to drink (not the healthiest but filling for little tummies). Something for the people. Just share lunch with them. There was one time when we went out, taking our tables and everything, we had a caravan of 26 vehicles going even further north to a part of Flint by Gracelawn Cemetery on Saginaw Street.

We met some other people who were out on the street praying for folks. One gal, who was kind of a street pastor, found us places to go each month and then her prayer warriors would be there to pray with the people and it was really cool so she would pick a spot and we would go there. She would show up in her car with a bullhorn and go up and down the streets and boom out to all the people that we were out there. It was incredible. We would come back mostly empty. The cleanup wasn't really hard at all. We would just pile up the tubs and then fill them up the next week.

I thought I had put my voices to rest. We met so many marginalized people on the street, I felt like we were in a third world country. We got to hear people's stories. We've even sat on the curbs to listen to people pour out their hearts to us. One woman comes to mind. She was extremely thin and not well. As a matter of fact, she had breast cancer and at home were her paraplegic husband and 12 children. They had just moved into a small home nearby. Prior to that they lived on the street or in abandoned buildings. They had no food, needed clothes and household items. This was in November, so Sister Carol took some volunteers back to St. Luke's Parish to get some items we don't usually carry with us. When she came back, the van was loaded, especially with lots of food and pots and pans, et cetera. The woman rode with Carol in the van. All the way to her house she sang songs of Thanksgiving to God. Her kids were very excited as they helped us unload. There was a 13 year old boy who walked Sister Carol to the van. He personally wanted to thank her.

That December we decided to surprise this family with food and gifts. When we arrived at the house, the same young man greeted Carol. She asked him to have some of the kids come out and help unload the van. His response was, "Oh no Sister, we don't need this help, but there is a family of 12 down the street who has nothing. Give these things to them." He pointed out the house. We were so impressed with this young man. We drove up to the house and the mom was outside with the dog. Sister Carol verified that we were at the right house and told the woman how we were directed her way. She burst into tears, hardly believing her blessing. She called the kids to empty the van and the more things they took in, the more excited they became.

Our parishioners always looked forward to our street stories. St. Luke's community was largely comprised of senior citizens and they supported the outreach ministry very well. One of our most moving experiences happened one January. A woman came by to see if there were any newborn baby clothes. Sister Carol brought out a storage tub of baby boy clothes. As the woman selected clothes, she related why she needed them. They were not for herself, but for a woman who had given birth to a baby, alone, in the abandoned house next to her.

When this woman got herself together, she wrapped her

newborn in her hoodie which was all that she had to keep herself warm. She went door-to-door looking for help. In Flint no one opens a door to a stranger at night. Fortunately, this lady did and she called an ambulance and went with her to Hurley Hospital. As it turned out, both mother and baby were miraculously doing well. They would be able to leave the hospital the next day, the day we were in the neighborhood. The clothes were for this little boy.

On the way back to the St. Luke's Sister Carol and I, almost simultaneously, said, "We need to do more for women and their children than just a band-aid of handouts. We need to change lives." The birth of that baby was the birth of the North End Women New Life Center. For years we wondered if one of the children coming to our food pantry was that little boy. Our street ministry ran for 5 years. When the streets became unsafe, we began to operate out of the school building that is now the St. Luke N.E.W. Life Center. We are still giving out clothing.

The voices continue to be there. They are in real time. They are voices on the phone and voices at our door. They keep coming and their issues are sometimes overwhelming, and I don't know how these people continue to survive. The one thing that they have is faith, much deeper than mine. They keep going for their children. They survive.

Sister Judy

I had met Sister Carol Weber OP, in 1984, when I changed from teaching grade school at St Pius X in Flint and began a parish ministry at St. Johns in Ypsilanti. I moved back to the Flint area in 1994 and ministered at St Agnes for 3 years with Fr. Cline and then for 2 years at St. Robert's in Flushing. Sister Carol had been appointed parish coordinator at St. Francis Xavier in Otisville and I lived with her there. I applied for and was hired as pastoral coordinator at St Luke's parish in the north end of Flint in 1994.

We got Sister Carol a part time job there. She joined me full time before the Bishop closed the parish in 2008.

St Luke's had its own grade school, operated by Sister Carol's order, the Adrian Dominican sisters, but the school closed and St Lukes leased the building to the Flint schools. When St. Luke parish closed we toured the school building with Bishop Boyea. Because of the magnitude of our ministry in the north end and the need for it to continue, the bishop let us use the school building. St. Luke N.E.W. Life Center was incorporated on September 10, 2008. Later the Bishop gave us the property as well.

A few years after we opened the Center, Jim Hutchins, who is the director of New Paths, (I was his teacher at St. Pius X Catholic School) called me and said "Can you help us out? The judge is releasing these women to us and we are hardly ready. The paint is not dried on the walls, but we need to add some programming. Can you help us during this time?" I said, "Yes." And St. Luke N.E.W. Life Center began working with the women from New Paths.

One day, during the many years we have had New Paths women at the Center, I had a very moving experience working with them. We were doing some kind of reflection and it just dawned on me, **"These are the faces, these are the women with blank faces, the nobodys, I've been dreaming about !"** And it was my little Jimmy from St Pius X 3rd grade who was the person that brought the women to us that clarified that whole thing.

MERCY

- **Forgiveness with no strings/conditions attached**

- **Forgiveness when the person "does not deserve forgiveness"**

- **God's mercy may seem unfair in our eyes—the nature of God's mercy is its excess, it balances nothing, is it not deserved**

- **Mercy is the force that re-awakens us to new life and instills in us the courage to look to the future with hope—it is a force that raises women and men up**

- **Ability to get inside other people until we can see things with their eyes, think things with their minds, feel things with their feelings**

Cara Manns (KK)

Cara Manns has a memory from when she was five years old. She is sitting in the back seat of a car with her mother and Big Jimmy in front. From between the bucket seats, she sees the man slip something into her mama's drink. Then the memory skips ahead to an ambulance taking her mother away, never to come home again. She can still remember the dress she wore to her mother's funeral, but she never remembers hearing anything about Big Jimmy being held accountable for her mother's death. Her mother was just gone.

"I always felt like my mother gave me away," Cara says. "But of course she didn't really. She died and my grandmother raised me and my three sisters. Four girls, grandma and my aunt all lived in a three bedroom apartment in the projects on Carpenter Road. Grandma got really involved at Carpenter Road Elementary

School where we were all enrolled. She attended schooling and parenting classes to get us off to a good start.

After elementary school I went on through junior high and into high school. My junior year, grandma got sick. She was partially paralyzed on her right side, so she couldn't do as much for herself any more. I figured, 'Well, she took care of me. I guess it's my time to help her,' so I dropped out of school and became her caregiver. I got a job in the customer service department of the Flint Journal so I could take care of grandma and earn some money for our household. When she died, l grew really depressed. She was the only mother I had really ever known.

When I was 18 I became a mother to my daughter, Cristle. Her dad and I lived together, but he was abusive and controlling. Often he would lock me inside the house to keep Cristle and me in. l used to love to see him leave for work, and I hated to see him come home. When he did, I would sit and watch him drink and fuss and complain. I'd drink with him until he'd pass out so I could feel calm. I used to pray that he would find another woman so I could be free.

Cara Manns (KK)

One day the abuse got so bad I couldn't stand it anymore. After he left for work, I lifted Cristle out a window that he hadn't locked. I lowered her to the ground, then climbed out myself and took her to a safe house. I never looked back, though I became friends with the woman he eventually married. She helped me raise Cristle.

After we escaped, I found work at a cleaning service where I stayed for four years. I made friends with a nice, calm man there named David. We had fun together and with our other coworkers, and eventually we fell in love. After about three years, we had Myeeah together, and David helped raise both my girls. Cristle still calls him Daddy.

Eventually I had to go on disability for my heart, and we were having a hard time making ends meet. The girls needed clothes, so I decided to visit St. Luke's N.E.W. Life Center. I remember Sister Judy told me they would be giving away food for Thanksgiving if I was interested, so I went back to get some food. But by the time I got there, it was all gone. Sister must have seen something in my eyes, because she reached into her pocket and pulled out a $20 bill. I remember she told me, 'Go buy your kids some milk.' That helped get us through.

A short time later I signed up for their Women's Group. One day each week for three years, I attended classes while my girls were in school. I learned about all kinds of things to make me successful in life from parenting to communication and budgeting to goal setting. It helped build my self esteem and set my sights on bigger goals.

I began to work on little jobs at the N.E.W. Life Center. Sometimes after I'd finish my work I just hung around, even after it was time to close. The sisters would say, "we're fixin' to go now," but I didn't want to leave.

Pretty soon I started to answer the phones at the main desk and I started taking classes to earn my GED. Some of those classes were hard, but the sisters tell us, "Can't is nothing. We don't know the word here and they're right! Barb White taught me math. Boy, she's a good woman. I couldn't believe I actually had fun learning it! And the sisters stayed on my back, like mothers, about getting that diploma. This is the best thing that could ever have happened to me.

Gosh the things the sisters have done for me! They taught me to sew and quilt, how to accept compliments and how to give to people. I didn't think I could make anything someone would pay for, but I sell blankets, quilts and fitted sheets at Octoberfest every year. When I was able to give another woman one of the blankets I made, Ha! It felt so good! I had always received before, but now I get to help someone else.

I'll never be in the system again. The sisters taught me to be self sufficient. Once I learned I could stand on my own, I got off disability and came to work at the N.E.W. Life Center. Before I got my GED, I saw myself as the woman who answers the phones. Once I earned my GED, I gave myself permission to say, 'Yep. I'm the receptionist now!' And when someone calls and says "I want to speak to KK," it makes me feel so good!

If I hadn't come here, I probably would have been drinking and drugging and stuff. Maybe selling a little drugs to keep a roof over my head. Now I'm able to know that I want a future. I want to go to college, take up a few classes so I can help other people the way the sisters have helped me. I don't think I ever want to leave this place. If could be a nun, I guess I would!

Do I have faith in Flint?" [There's a note of surprise] "Do l have faith in Flint? Oh my! Yes. Yes, I do because I've learned that people put up walls not to keep others out, but to see who cares enough to tear them down. There are lots of problems — schools closing, crime all over, but everyone's not bad. There are good people out there who can help if you let them. That's another lesson I learned at St. Luke's."

[KK became a wonderful volunteer, telling her story to service clubs, parishes in many cities and anywhere it would help the Center. Her smile and big laugh were joy itself. Unfortunately her health got worse and she had to stop coming to the Center. Sister Carol wasn't available to take her call, so she left this message]:

"Good morning, Sister Carol this is KK. I was calling to let you know, um, I won't be in at all this week. I'm doing, pul.. pul.. pulamonary rehabilitation. I'm starting to have negative thoughts and stuff about this whole COPD thing. Read about it and now it's just, I guess I don't want just kicking in it if there's no cure for this.

Now they're, [sobs] I'm gonna be doing some training to see how, to help me know how to manage dealing with it. So I'm going to be doing, um, like, um, psychological counseling, um, nutritional things and exercises and stuff that may help me cope with this and not be so negative. [snufffles] But I'll be up there Tuesday. I think it's Tuesday to talk to, um, to you. Cause um, I did receive my paperwork from, um, the disability place and they said, um, if that I won't, my doctor said I'm not able to work and that, um, if I work, then I'm not disabled. So [cries] I'll just, um, I'll give you a call back a little later to talk to you.

Thank you. Bye bye."

Julie Chuchvara

New Paths women come every Wednesday, nine to three. They're at New Paths as an alternative to jail or prison due to substance abuse or a nonviolent crime. Some of them are there voluntarily, a small percentage. Wednesday is just like kind of a bonus day to just get out of there and have kind of like a nice day for women. They do knitting and crocheting. Sometimes they'll do a craft or a game. They might watch a movie. They read out of the Resisting Happiness book, do Bible studies and they do a lot of talking about issues.

And it's a good way for them to get help. They can access the DHHS worker, the lawyer, me [a social worker] if they have questions or problems and we can give them the resources to help. Also while they're here, we let them know about our employment prep program and the other stuff that we have going on here like the Literacy Center. Because when they get out it's a way for them to know about a resource, a safe place to go, something that they've been to and they've seen that they can come to when they get out. And we have had quite a few women sign up for the employment prep while they're in there so that they have something set up. So as soon as they get out, they know they're coming here. So there's not that gap where they might relapse. And that's been really important.

Women from New Paths (part 1)

Christina: The father of my children passed away about a year ago and his parents filed for custody about three days after. They got an ex parte motion, you know, I don't have to be there, know about it and they can just talk all this talk, whether it's true or not. And I couldn't even defend myself. Well, they got my kids for four days out of the week and I get them for three, but it's only considered grand-parenting time. So I just want to know why they have so many rights just for grand-parenting time.

I mean, I didn't keep the kids away from [them] cause they go to church with them and stuff. And you know, I, after he passed away, I stepped up to the plate and I got myself a full-time job and I was actually doing pretty good. Like I went back in with my mom. So there is a roof over their heads. I had the Bridge Card at the time. So they had food, they had everything they were supposed to have. And I still got the short straw.

I need a lawyer and the thing is I'm supposed to be to court tomorrow, but I can't leave [New Paths].

Adrean: You can leave for court.

Christina: Ah, they told me I couldn't. I called my probation agent and she told me...

Adrean: I'd go down there and see if you can get an order. You know what I mean?

Christina: Because that was like the first thing I said to her...

Adrean: I'd be talking to everybody in that courthouse.

Christina: I'm like, well, it's been a mess. And that's kinda why I spiral, spiral down as bad as I did because it was kind of like, no matter how hard I was trying, it was just not, I was getting nowhere real fast, like, so yeah, kind of.

Say my addiction, I just spiraled out of control. I ended up losing my job because you know, like I kind of felt like too, like, you know, me stepping up to the plate and having my kids to keep myself structured like that. And I just felt like that was kind of ripped away from me. And then their dad was, you know, unexpectedly passed away and a lot of things were going on in my life.

It's not like I was, you know, not letting their grandparents see him and it's not like, like it was nothing like that. And she keeps saying over trying to help you. But I mean like you wait for me to ask you for help, you know? Like you don't sit there and just try to take over my kids. So yeah.

I've been in New Paths since Tuesday. Last Tuesday. So it hasn't been long at all, but it all just kind of, cause yeah, I didn't know I was going to get sent in here and then I had the means to take care of it. But then I got sent here and that kind of threw me a curve ball and didn't really know what to do. I got 90 days.

I'm really trying to stay sober and maintain my sobriety. Like I've only been to one other treatment place before this and I wasn't quite ready. But I'm ready now because it's just, it's tiring and it's definitely not making my situation any better. So yeah, it's a struggle. Coming to St Luke's helps because it's teaching me like, you know, things I don't know how to do. It makes me feel kind of better about myself talking to all these ladies here. And it's definitely positive here. It's more positive. And I like this place a lot. It's my first time being here and I really do like it a lot.

Adrean: This is what we look forward to all week. You know, I've always said, I've always believed in God. I was raised Catholic. Um, but it was more of a holiday, saint's days, you know, go to mass then. Um, and you know, sitting through Bible studies and stuff, it was just so boring to me and I'd be like falling asleep and I couldn't hear anything. I love Ms. Gaytra's Bible studies. She just explains things so you can understand it. Um, the ladies are so helpful and appreciative of us being here. Who wants to be around us? You know what I mean? Um,

Jeanne: It's so peaceful. This is just a wonderful place. There's so much going on. There's so much going on for the community and the food's good too.

Regina: I've eaten more of the spaghetti and possibly even the meat than anywhere. The food's much better. Yeah. This place is a blessing. It is definitely.

Adrean: This was my, actually my fourth time going through treatment because I was in treatment when I was 15, um, as well. Um, but I really believe the reason I didn't succeed is because I wasn't taking God seriously. I didn't have a relationship with God. I'm finally starting, you know? And when people talk about believing in God and a relationship with God it's like, you don't know the difference, I think until you actually start getting a relationship with God. It took me a long time. I feel different. I know I got this. I don't want to live that life. I'm good. This is what I need.

Ever since I can remember from being a small child, you know, my mom was an alcoholic. She had mental problems, she was a drug addict. And from the time I was in elementary school, I was like, Oh, I can't wait to put that straw up my nose. I can't wait to smoke weed. I can't wait to drink. You know what I mean? When I get big enough. And when I was 14, my mom started paying me and my friends cocaine to babysit my younger siblings. So she started, you know, um, my house was a party house. Everybody in high school would come to party at my house as long as they brought drugs or alcohol or money.

Um, and as soon as I started, you know, when I got pregnant, I quit everything. Um, I was clean for about 10 years. Didn't do anything because I didn't want my kids to know that life. I never let them meet my mother. Um, and I went to nursing school. I was registered nurse for 24 years. After about 10 years being clean, I did start taking pain pills. I was hooked on pain pills, but I wouldn't admit it. You know, I didn't, I'm not addicted. I have pain since I'm running around all day. Story of my life.

Um, and I got into a bad car accident in 2010, broke my back in three places, had injury, crushed my hip. And it was about a year recovery time. Um, before, you know, everything kinda came back together, but that was just another excuse. And I completely spiraled out of control. I started using heroin, crack, drinking every day. Um, not sleeping. I had a heart attack two years ago. That didn't even stop me. I didn't care.

And you know, I've went to treatment a couple of times. It's at the point now where my kids want nothing to do with me because they don't understand it. They weren't raised around that stuff. Um, I'm finally building relationships with my daughter and my middle son. Again, my youngest son isn't ready. I have four grand babies. The oldest one I've seen twice and he's three. I think that says a lot. [breaks down crying] It's OK cause I got this this time. I know what I want. I know what I want.

I did almost three years in Alderson, West Virginia federal prison and six months in a halfway house for drugs. Yes. [I got sent to New Paths after] another drug felony. Yeah. And you know, even after that I didn't even care. I sat in jail for five weeks. We had already reached an agreement: two years probation. Went to court and I was bound and determined when I get out of here,

I'm really going to get messed up - party on. And the judge threw 90 days New Paths at me. I had no intention of staying there. Not for one day. I wasn't going to walk in the building. I was getting picked up as soon as I walked in the parking lot. And I don't know what a feeling just came over me. And I'm like, you know what? You just need to give this 24 hours. And the next day you need to give this another 24 hours. And just being around people like me that actually wanted to get their lives together. And, you know, seeing positive things and their kids are coming to see him. Um, I don't know, something. I just, I just want my family.

[The feeling that came over you?] You know, and I swear this is God. I swear. Just like goosebumps just to, um, like my chest was just so full. Like I was so full. Um, and I think I finally realized what I was doing. You know, I thought that was what was making me happy. Like I didn't even care. My kids didn't talk to me. I didn't care. I was okay before I had you. I'm okay now. But then this feeling came over me.

You know, I was always such a good mother and they think I've completely lost my mind. That I'm mentally insane. Like you need to be locked in a mental hospital. We don't know what's wrong with you, but there's something wrong with you. When I was using yeah. You know, and they're just starting to come around. I mean, it hasn't even been 60 days that I have been clean yet. Um, but I can honestly tell you that feeling that I got as the same feeling, um, that I got, what I think I finally realized I was starting a relationship with God. When I pray, I get goosebumps and I just, it's a joy, uh, a happiness that I, I, I can't even explain. I don't know.

I do Our Father. Um, I might throw a rosary in once in a while. Um, I just talked to God. Every night when I'm laying in bed at least 20 minutes. I talk to God until I fall asleep. About everything. And let Him kind of talk to me. I don't remember if it was last night or the night before, you know, I always say, tell my mom and my grandma, my Nana, see them soon and I miss them and I wish they were here just one more hour. And my Nana's face like flashed in my head. So, like she was standing right there.

Jeanne: Like a spiritual awakening?

Adrean: I think so. I was crying. I'm like, Oh my goodness, this has never happened before. Like what the heck? All these, I don't cry. And I'm crying all the time now. And I mean, I have absolutely no doubt about it. That's why I haven't succeeded before in recovery. Um, I didn't have a relationship with God and I didn't think I'd have one. I mean, I've been working at it and just one day it was just like there. I got it. Oh, I got it. I know what I want. I know what I have to do. I know what I'm going to do. I'm going to continue to do it and that's it. And if it wasn't for New Path—I'm just so thankful I gave myself 24 hours to stay there because I had no intention. I didn't care if I was going to go back to jail. I didn't care if I was going to go back to prison. I'm going to party.

When I get done with New Paths I will still be coming to St Luke's all the time. It's peaceful here? Everybody I've met is so helpful. Miss Gaytra is my new mother. [Gaytra Molinari a volunteer at the Center] You know, we learned a lot of things to do like, my big thing is boredom and I'm learning so many new things here to keep my mind busy, to keep my hands busy. Um, if I need a prayer, I can open the door and anybody walking by, you know, I need to get a new skill. I want it to go back to work. I think that would be the beginning of having a normal life again. So I mean, that program [St Luke's] would benefit me. Okay. All right. I've already told you, you're stuck with me. I'll be back.

Christina: I used to work at the Grand Traverse Pie Company. So [a baking program at St Luke's] is really up my alley. They started me out as the deli clerk. I, you know, like cut the meats and weighed them out for those sandwiches and did the soups and all that. But I was the first one, out of people that worked there for like five years, that did the deli and the bakery. I'd come in and start baking at like five, six o'clock in the morning. I'd have like a two, three hour break and come back and do the deli. But yeah, I loved every minute of it.

Because when you can enjoy what you're doing, because the last job I had that I messed up, I was working at CarRite. And I was taping up the cars for them to be painted, which was like really cool. But at the same time, being a single mom, going through everything that I was going through, it was like a lot of hours. And it was really laborus. I was always tired when I did have my kids, but I still wasn't using as much as I did towards the end.

Jeanne: You go downhill so fast. You just can't, even nobody that's had an addiction, doesn't understand. It's all fun and games. And then you wake up one day and it's like, wow, that happened quick.

Christina: For me to completely hit rock bottom it took about a month, if that. If that cause like, you know, I had my addiction, I was like maintaining low. Like I'd, you know, I'd get high and drink when my kids were gone for those four days. And then the three days that I had them I didn't do anything. I might have a couple of drinks where I go to bed when they're already in bed. But it just started getting to the point where things were supposed to work out a certain way and they didn't.

This is my first time at St. Luke N.E.W. Life Center. I love this place. I'm definitely gonna come back. Everyone's like... I love this place. It's really awesome. I'm actually thinking about going to church and stuff here when I can leave again. Cause I grew up Catholic and stuff. So, and, uh, for some reason, like they're making a big deal about church in the front of the court. Like it actually, cause you usually don't mix church and court. But for some reason, since my kids go to church three days a week with their grandparents, like, it's just, I'm like, well, I can take them to church too, but I mean like, it's going to be on some days and maybe like catechism on Wednesdays or something. I don't know if that's still how it goes, but whenever it is. Yeah, yeah. I can do that too, definitely.

Deb T.

[Volunteers at the Center to Deb: "We can help you with your immediate needs today, for sure."] Okay. Yeah. I just brought my son, Marcus, he's about to be 13, to school at Hamady. I was sitting there [at the bus stop] trying to... how am I going to get some diapers? My baby is two months. He just turned two months old. Okay. Christian Leo [G.....]and I only gave him a middle name, Leo, because he was born right at the end of Leo season. He weighed 7 pounds eight ounces. He's 13 pounds now. He only got two diapers. I sat at the corner bus stop and I was sitting there crying. I was like, God... then I looked, I seen the truck. It said," Women's Center". I said," Let me go see if they can help me."

[In the past] I'll go down to the Women's Answer Center sometimes, but they only help you once a month. And um, they help when he was born, they go help me again at six months. And they got me a pack-and-play and they got me, um, car seat. I wouldn't even been able to bring him home [from the hospital] without the car seat. So they helped me with that. And then, but they don't help with like baby food and stuff and stuff like that. And I was like, okay. I asked her do they help with Christmas help. She said, if I qualified for the program, I'm on section eight. That's low income. But they right where they're building that new ramp and apartments downtown on Second. They say they're going to tear it down.

And so I was just at the bus stop and the truck said" Women's Center". And I said, that sounded like love incorporated or something. I'm like, okay, let me go in there and see. And it's a blessing.

[Deb left with formula and diapers for the baby, clothes for all three boys and herself. She planned to come back the next day for lunch and the food distribution from the pantry after she dropped Marcus off at Hamady for school. She was going to bring her 2 year old son as well so he could become more social]

Sharon M.

Police report I got that done. He got put in jail. The police saw the marks that night. My elbows and arms are all scratched up and black and blue. I have two black eyes. My whole body is pretty much bruises and scrapes and scraps. [but you haven't been to the doctor yet. Get a CT scan done.] I don't know. I've had dizzy spells before. Eventually they go away. He took my wallet and my phone. I just want him to leave me alone. After it happened I had gotten sick sitting on the sidewalk. I was sitting in there for a few minutes and this lady saw me and gave me a ride home. Got me Thanksgiving dinner. Gave me pepper spray when she saw what was done to me. And she's like, here, take this pepper spray. It was only five, it only cost me five bucks. You need it more than I do. Alright. I make sure I keep that with me. Even in the house, like whichever room on me, my keys are with me. Cause he still got keys to the house.

He claimed to love me. And then when I said I didn't love him and didn't want to be with him anymore, that's when he attacked. He kept repeating are you ready to let me love you? Are you ready to let me love you again? That's not love. I kept telling him BS, you don't love me. Not if you treat me like crap. You don't love me. You're going to call me every name in the book including out on the street. He tells me just walking around in stuff like this, jeans and a T-shirt, makes me look like a hooker. I'm not wearing all that body makeup. I'm not sitting there lifting my shirt up on the road. I'm walking around, minding my own business. You don't have to defend yourself on that one.

Nope. I'm not going back to him, he's not coming back. Once you physically hit me, there is no going back. I'm going to call my cousin to see if she can get me some extra support as soon as I can get my phone back or get my ID so I can use the computer at the library. And that would be good. I'm going to walk downtown to the jail to see if I can get my phone and my wallet. I have to be walking 'cause I'm not supposed to be driving my car. He was in jail for a month. He had just gotten out of 14th of last month. He had just gotten out and then ended up back in there less than two weeks later.

Some friends of mine that I met up at the library up the road brought me here. They've been coming here for lunch. Okay. And they met me one day. Brought me here and I've been coming here for about a month and a half. I'm just helping out 'cause I wanted something to do. I came here expecting lunch and I didn't know they were doing Christmas presents. Okay. Can I stay and help? That isn't sitting at home by myself getting more and more depressed and little more anxiety. I had brought him here a couple times. I thought it might be a positive influence and do him some good. But it didn't work out.

Gaytra and Liz register families for food distribution

COMPASSION

- "The most important thing in the life of every man and every woman is not that they should never fall along the way, the important thing is to get back up." Pope Francis

- Feeling for and desiring good for a person that is so strong with you that you feel it in your gut

- Compassion is about justice—being in right relationship

- Expression of true solidarity, esp. with poor and oppressed—personal commitment to act in such a way that it relieves another's suffering from injustice that causes pain and keeps another in oppressive & degrading situations

- Sharing one-another's joys and successes

- What happens to another, whether it be a joy or a sorrow, happens to me.

Lisa Hirsch

So, about 10 years ago, my husband and I started bringing groups of families to Flint to do service work. We would come on a Sunday, have Mass and then Monday, Tuesday and Wednesday we would work. One of the sites that came to was St. Luke's N.E.W. Life Center and we met Sister Carol and Sister Judy. Our former pastor, Father Tom Firestone, is now the Pastor here in Flint and so our church, St. Mary's Student Parish in Ann Arbor had been sending students to Flint for alternative spring break. My husband and I thought that it would be great to bring families here, in the summertime, sort of an alternative summer break.

So we called Father Tom and said what do you think about this and he said, "Sure, I talked to my friend, Dave Wolpert, to see if you can stay at his house." So we stayed with Dave Wolpert for several years and then one year we were a little too big, so we stayed at the convent, I think at Holy Family Church, in Grand Blanc. I am trying to remember now, and then when the Firestone

Center opened, we have been staying there the last 3 or 4 years. It's up at St. Mike's in the old rectory.

In 2019, we had 41 people in our group so a couple of the families actually stayed with Dave because we couldn't all fit at the Firestone Center. And we always, so we do go to other places to do work, but we always come as a full group and on the last day, we always work at St. Luke's together, because I want everybody to see St. Luke's and have Sister or Kay give the new people a tour every year that we work there.

We do whatever Sister Carol or Sister Judy wants us to do. We've done everything from yard work, cleaning up, pulling weeds, raking, painting the parking blocks out front, we have done getting things ready for the Christmas distribution, putting large bottles of soap or shampoo or conditioner into small bottles so they can be put into toiletry bags, moving things, doing all kinds of things. Whatever is needed. Working in the pantry....

So, we come with those families once a year and then we also have a group that comes around before Christmas time, our Parish has something called "Our feast day of service." It is around the Feast of Immaculate Conception, which is St. Mary's feast day. We bring a group then as well and then we also usually, my husband and I come up a little bit later, closer to Christmas, and bring things from our Advent Giving Tree that we also do for St. Luke's and St. Mary's.

Antonio McNeal

I just love it here. They help me out, so I am like helping the people that God is loving since they gave me a chance, I like helping other people. So, my thing is, I would rather be here with them and help them out and try to make they still grow more. I would rather help take care other people like they helped take care of me and my family.

And I love it here and I have even asked them to teach me how to sew. They haven't taught me yet, but I am hoping they do. Just want to learn something new just in case, if they need me down there, I would like to go down there and help them out too.

That is a loving and caring place and you will be successful in some way, somehow. You will learn, you will get use out of this program. Oh, we will accept any volunteer. We won't turn them down. And we got some work for them to do.

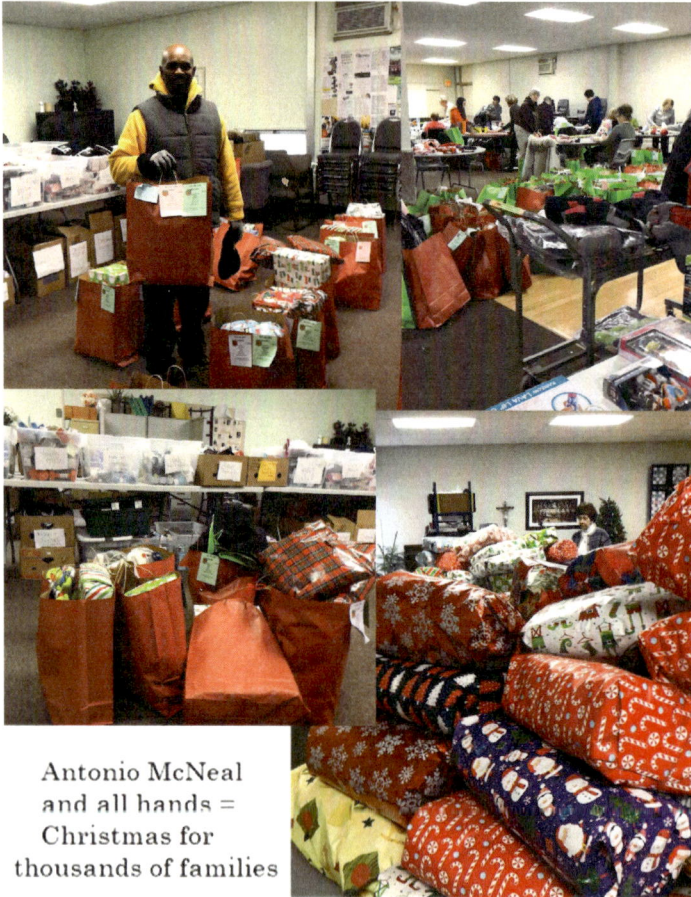

Antonio McNeal and all hands = Christmas for thousands of families

And I met a lot of people from being here. A lot of people I never see before I met but now when I see them outside I still talk to them and usually I wouldn't do that but from being here, now when I see, like if I see you outside, I would stop you and talk to you, usually I wouldn't do that. Yes, being here made me feel, yep, made me feel a way lot better about myself.

Uh huh and my kids love it too. Instead of me just sitting at home all the time, waiting on them to get out of school, trying to help them, they learned that I am getting out and I am working, it makes them want to work, so, when I get home they try to help me in the yard and stuff. And then they want to work too, they get the idea that they should be developing themselves so that they can find a job, which is better for them. I got some good respectful kids and I got two kids in college right now.

We try to teach them the best way we can. And when they come up here, they help out. I have them working with me, like you all have to do something, you aren't just going to sit around, you know? You aren't going to do something, well you have to go get a book and read, just to keep their mind together instead of just wanting to play and be all big because of all the technology now that all the kids be on and they don't want to do anything but be on the games or check on their phone

I try to make sure everybody leaves here with a smile on their face, at least, instead of looking all mad. And I mingle with everybody too so I can tell you who most of the customers are when they come in, what size family they have because I talk to them. The people, that's why they always calling my name because I mingle with them, talk to them, I know their name, they know my name, so, yeah, I try to make them feel happy and warm when they are here.

Paul Bagwell

I come around here full-time back in about May, maybe about August [2019], not sure. It was in between going back down there. More back and forth running.

My Aunt Rosemary got me to the Center in the first place. She is here volunteering. My Cousin Maria is a volunteer as well and I was just sitting around the house and they told me to come on up. I did that men's group and all that. I am part of the lawn crew during the summer times. Do a lot of mowing over at Applewood and other people's lawns and at the blight down neighborhoods. We keep pretty busy, doing a little bit of everything.

Yeah, I do all of that and I just do all of this now and it is all pretty good, you know? Today is food distribution day so I gotta get back into the pantry. Everybody is treated real good around here, pretty good times. Just keep busy....I gotta go.

Rhonda Fitzsimmons

I came here to volunteer rather than just sitting at home. Sister Judy asked me to hand out lunch tickets on Tuesdays, Thursdays. Anybody who just comes in off the street, anybody. Anybody can come get lunch. They get identified or something just so we know who they are. Well, they have a lunch sign-in sheet. So they sign there. Then I get them the lunch ticket. Then they take it over to the kitchen area. I tell people grab a chair and sit with me. So they'll sit with me and they'll bring their lunch and talk. And it's like, let's go ahead, whatever it takes to just [have] some human interaction. Some, yeah. Just somebody. People care about each other. You know? What a wonderful place.

I mentor New Paths women on Wednesdays, too. The Bible study, Gaytra does that part. We do exercises and we go to one of the rooms and the volunteers there teach them knitting and crocheting. Like, I just, you know, I just try to encourage them. Yes. I just tell him, you know, l want you to succeed. And they don't hear that from anybody. Yeah, yeah. That's what they say.

I was at Dorothy's House last week. Okay. Because people know I work up here [at the Center], I sit there and have to answer questions. That's all right. Because that gets the story out. It's just, I just love this place. It's so much fun and there's so many good things going on and these people in the area, I don't know what they would do for food and clothes. No, I just don't know what they would do if this place wasn't here.

Women from New Paths (part 2)

Regina: I just like, I'm not a real big talker cause I was an only child. But I like it. I love coming here, I gets up stewed every day waiting for this day to come so I can come here. And plus that's my Granny G [Gaytra].

And I'm like, I'm here with, uh, what is my roomy now? I reads the Bible every night with my flashlight. I don't care, if I get to read my Bible it keeps me going. And then when I come here, she do it. I went to school. I graduated, but I didn't graduate. I paid people to do my work at school. So I'm coming back here and she told me, I come here with her and get my GED. And I'm not really a female person, but she made me so comfortable that I love it here. I was really a tomboy, you know. I didn't know the mother, the female stuff. I did all the male stuff. But I'm getting there, little by little.

I sold drugs, did drugs, I did with all the male things that they say pimps do. I was the female male version. You know, I didn't never depend on nobody. I did what I had to do and just survive. And my kids, they grew up good without they father. Cause I did the manly thing to show my people about me. Like my grandkids. They made all my grandkids,15 boys and 2 girls.

I love it. Coming here. I look forward to coming here. It makes me, it makes my, makes my time and New Path go faster. Cause I know I, I coming up here to see my granny, you know, Wednesday, every Wednesday I got visitation when my grandma. Not behind bars, I'm with my grandma out in the world.

[How did you run into trouble with the law?]

Actually, I turned myself in, after I beat this dude up, I threw him into the cooler and snatched him out and he went into the washer powder. And when the washer powder went up, it fell on me. He started sneezing. I could've got away, but I didn't. I stopped cause I was raised to say, bless you. And I kept saying bless you. And he kept sneezing.

He came in the gas station looking for, He said, where'd that girl go. And I'm like, Hi. In another world I have seven personalities. So that came out. The one that came out was, you know, the sport brat, you know. Daddy's baby mama's maybe we be in the hood. And when I see them walk by, so you looking for me and he had to ding up and I pushed him in there. Then he like tried to turn around and I snatched him and he went into the middle aisle where the washing powder and bleach and stuff is. When his big butt fell... but it shocked me that I really grabbed him like that. And he fell and the wash powder came up and he like [sneezes]. Bless you.

I was walking down the street. He kept saying, Hey, you want a date? I said, no, but you want to know what day it is I tell you. You know, I'm just like that. I'm very outspoken. He kept calling me B, omething' like that. I'm like, dang, how you know my name? You know, I do stuff. Cause you're not going make me mad. Right. I might've tried to get me a hustle. He was nothing but my day, you know. So he ended up coming in and I was like, I don't know how I'm going to do it but let's get this going. Cause if he touch me, you know, I'm going to kick him in his knee or snatch his Adam's apple or something. Because I was walking away. My father always taught me. The big gonna walk away. But you going to be the man. Cause I got three older brothers and three younger brothers. Now I'm in the middle. So all that, you hit me in my chest and stuff, that don't work, you know. You can call me out my name, I'm not going to cry. I ain't going to call nobody saying he doing this. I'm a do it. You know?

So like the police officers were like, when they turned in I say, come on. I'm ready to go. And then that's when the gas station said, come here, come here, come here. And then she said hold on. I was like, okay. Cause I thought she actually called with the dude's girlfriend card. And he said, you could have been gone. You know? And they kept looking, watching. I stood there almost two hours while they kept watching the CCTV video.

I was walking out. I was walking out and then they told me, I said, here I go, I'm ready. But they really weren't coming. They didn't know what happened. She had ended up calling off her cell phone. So when they told me to wait, I waited, I ain't gonna to run. I was too tired. He was like, you know, you could have been gone [if you didn't stop to say God Bless you]. If you wouldn't have stopped. I said, "Well, I have warrants anyway. I'm ready to go to sleep. I'm tired."

But if I wouldn't have stopped to say, "God bless you," to the guy sneezing, I would've left the station and been outa there. Yeah. But I was raised that way. If somebody sneeze, say, God bless you.

And this guy started gagging. And that's what I seen the little blue liquid. He had the fabric softener and the dryer sheets and everything on him. And I thought he was choking and gonna to die. So I, you know, that's real bad when you did a murder. I watch too much CSI criminal minds. As long as you can prove that when you left they was living, it's not held a crime. You're not held.

So I say you alright. He said, yeah. I left, was gonna let it go. They stopped me. I seen he was breathing when I left so whatever happened after that was not on me. And when I went to court and I told them, they was laughing, You know. Judge Kelly, she was laughing. But she was like, you, you, you really, you gonna to New Path. And I got anger management classes. I was on the New Path property before, but this time I went in because she told me if you don't, I'm sending you to prison. So I'm not going back in front of her. I got to do 90 days. I'm doing my 90 days and come back and take my paper to her stating I complete it.

Then I'm coming here cause I got certificates too. And I gotta have my grandma G. I feel safe in here. I feel safe. I'm comfortable with it. Cause we get my GED, this, I got to high school. I graduated with honors, but I didn't graduate. She was the smart one, whatever she wanted. I had just write that paperwork out now, write it in my own head. Right. But I'm going to do it myself this time. The day I get outa here I'm a signing up. They told me I could. [For the literacy GED program]

Jeanne: Um, well my probation officer, she sent me there [to New Paths] cause I'd just done almost 60 days at Sacred Heart out in Memphis. I completed twice. My probation officer said she wanted me to do six months residential with a 30 day review. Well, it's been past 30 days, no review. I had court on the 13th for my son because when I was in rehab, cause I just, after being clean for a year and six months, I had just tried heroin for the first time because I couldn't get my Xanax. And um, I told my mom, I didn't know, I felt like I was dying. And I went to go pack my clothes the next day. And the police were at the door. CPS was at the door and my mom called my probation agent. And my mom just pretty much set me up for failure.

Even though I can't say my mom set me. I set myself up for failure by relapsing after being a year in six months. And um, so I used on January 1st and um, by January 7th I was in rehab. And then on the 10th, my son was taken away from me. My mom got temporary guardianship. And then when my probation officer had told me she wants me to do six months residential with a 30 day review. It's going on almost 60 days. I had court on the 13th. They extended the temporary guardianship for six more months until I can get a job and a house and then I can petition the court and get my kid back. So then I had to report to probation after court and my probation officer, I thought she was gonna let me do outpatient, cause I had just come successfully completed rehab twice. Short term, of course, but it's still better than nothing.

And um, so she sent me straight to New Path and I've been here since the 13th. And um, my probation officer looks at me and treats me like a drug addict instead of a human being. And I don't feel like she is out for my best interest. I had asked her if I could see my kid, cause my mom's like you can come see him every single day of the week, four to eight. And then she's like,

I have to talk to your mom about that. So the eight year old and a three year old, this is the longest time I've ever been without my kids. This last 60 days. I've always been a goodass mom. Pardon my French. Now my probation officer's saying she didn't answer me back about seeing my two oldest boys. She said she was calling my mom and I'm supposed to be doing this program until recovery housing is available. Okay. So whenever recovery housing is available then I'll be able to go with recovery housing. Right. Um, and then I plan on part of the program for up to a year just so I can hold my head on.

Because before this year and six months, I was sober. I had relapsed on my benzos, and my Xanax and I was clean for five years. And then before that it was two years. I had really bad PTSD after I had my son and I was molested at three years old and raped by my uncle. My mom's been out of my life. My mom hasn't been a part of my life for seven years before this last year and five years before that. So like my mom becomes part of my life and it's like, I'm getting slammed. I need Xanax, I need something. So I need to protect my boundaries and cut my mom off completely because it seems like every time she comes to my life, I don't know if I just hold me getting abused by my uncle or, you know, her being drunk and high at a party when my leg got broken when I was five years old. You know I don't know if I just hold her accountable for that. And I just don't. I'm just glad I'm out with my mom. That's what led me here. So I'm hoping. I think it's going to work this time. I believe so. It's hard to say what the future holds.

Adrean: Well, about a year after my car accident, I got so hooked on Oxycontin. Um, you know, so of course my prescription would be gone··· 150 pills within two weeks and I was, you know, having withdrawal so bad. My friend was like, here do this line of heroin. And I was like, Oh, I'd never known anybody that did it, sold it; never seen it. No. And then, I mean, within 12 hours I was calling just come over and give it to me. If it'll make me feel better. I was off and running. I got necrotizing fasciitis in my arm. I almost lost my arm. I'm cut from my wrist, my elbow, and halfway up from necrotizing fasciitis I got from needles. I was in the hospital for six weeks. I had three surgeries. They, every time I went into surgery, the doctor told me, I don't know if you're going to wake up with an arm. It depends on what it looks like when I get in there. Nobody came to the hospital.

Dirty needles. I just use my needles over and over, I was a registered nurse. I know better, but I'm like using alcohol on my skin. You know what I mean?

I quit doing heroin every day about three to four years ago. And a year ago I moved in, well I moved in with him longer ago than that. He was only selling crack. Then he started selling heroin. So I started dabbling a little bit, doing a line here and there. Um, and of course hanging around certain people. I'd shoot up like once a week. Guess what? Necrotizing fasciitis in my thigh. This was just in September. I'm cut from here to here. I was in the hospital for two weeks at time, had a wound vac. The scars on my leg are horrible. Almost lost my leg. It's just, it's crazy. Absolutely crazy. I'm, I'm tired. I'm done. No doubt about it. God's got me. That's the only person that's got me.

People take such advantage because, and I'm not saying this is everybody. It's the group of people I was around. Like they would spend their social security check, getting high and then not pay rent or consumers. And they're going to all these agencies and churches to get all their stuff paid when people that are really struggling... you know what I mean? Really need it. Yeah. Yeah. I used to be there. I was right there. When I went to Meridian my mom spent my $509 off of my bridge card and her $370 off her bridge card and you know, trading it for crack in about three days. I was so, I wanted to rip her head off so bad.

There's not a lot of places that will help you as much as you guys help people here. No, when you, if you get a tour, you are not going to believe everything they have going on here. The first day

I got here, I got a quick little and I was just like, wow. I mean, they are really for the community and helping people. We are seeing a free eye doctor tomorrow. Free. Yeah. Everyone I've met like genuinely really cares. And your Bible studies are the best. Like I understand what you're saying. Maybe it's just that I wasn't paying attention before because I'd let my mind wander. And I'd be thinking about this and that and trying to go to sleep.

And like she said, it's so safe here. Yeah. It's like, nobody wants to hurt you. Everybody wants to help you here. Everybody wants to see you succeed. Right now. I feel like I'm fighting everybody on the outside. She can't do it. She can't do it. I'm going to prove y'all wrong. I'm going to prove all y'all wrong. I don't care if I have to move into the church.

Charlita Walker

I beat cancer three times since I have been here. I have had a heart recorder put in my chest, three years I was supposed to wear that for 6 months where my heart was skipping beat. I lost my parents and my brothers, they are my family. All of this stuff was happening to me, which was Satan trying to break me down and it all happened and because I am annoying that he can't do nothing with me so he tries to put things on me but I always bounce back up. Because there is nothing he can do with me.

You can pray for me all day long but whatever, I have to have that within me. You know what I mean? Because if I just give up because I am sick or whatever, just goes and withers up and die, it isn't going to happen with me. I am a fighter. Yes I am. Looking at me you wouldn't even think that.

I come here and share it, that is what it is about. Not giving up no matter what your circumstances look like, it's the end to things. Especially anything bad is an end to it. But you got to believe and have that faith. God has you. That's all that is to it.

That is for sure. God can do anything but you got to believe and have that faith. You do.

I am here every day, Monday through Friday, I am here from 8-4, every day I am here, you see Charlita, in this office (to buzz people in the door) or something they can't get in because I am down there somewhere. I do all kinds of stuff. Donations, wherever I can help at. But mostly, I have been here so I have to do donations, answer the phone, let the people in, take the clothes down in the basement for donations. Whatever I can do that they need me to do that I am available to do, that is what I do. Anything to help the Center. That is what I do.

I first came here back in 2013 or 2012. I think it was 2012, actually. I had been coming up here. I found out about the Center through a friend of mine who used to come here to volunteer. I was working in a nursing home. So I started coming up on Saturdays because they used to have a food program that they feed people on Saturdays, every Saturday, me and Shirley would come up here and help, do whatever we could do to help out.

So Sister Carol asked me, she told me about the sewing program that they were going to get going on. So I ended up, I was still working at a nursing home, I was working 3rd shift, I would come here on that Tuesday, go to that class and that's how I got involved was for the class, to do that sewing and that's how I got in to learn how to become a professional sewer. I think back then it was maybe 12 weeks. Anyway, you had to come.

I was hired as a sewer, well not right after graduation, that because I was still working in the nursing home. I had been at the nursing home for 15 years working in the medical field. I ended up hurting my back so badly I came out of that field, a slipped disc in my back and I can't lift patients anymore. But you know, I couldn't let that get me down.

Oh, while I worked in the sewing room and Cara got sick. I was substituting for her instead of being out in the sewing room and when she comes back I will be up here on Mondays and Fridays. But I like working up here with the people because of the things that I see make me more grateful, you know, how blessed I am. You know what, you never know what a person is going through, you never know what you can say to rise the person up, you never know. Never know what's going through them, what they need. I am a hugger. I like to hug people. That is just me. That is how I was brought up. To respect everybody. Everybody deserves respect. That is how I was brought up.

Julie Chuchvara

Right now I'm here as a social worker with the employment preparation program. It's 16 weeks, one day a week of class, nine o'clock to three. The women are on Tuesdays and the men are on Thursdays. And then they volunteer on their opposite days. And in order to graduate from the program, they have to get 30 hours of volunteer service, pass the drug test and not miss more than two classes and be working on their GED. They've either never had a job or have had trouble carrying a job for a long period of time. Every one of them has lots of barriers, things that have held them from jobs before. It could be transportation, evictions, substance abuse, domestic abuse, mental health. You know, and many people have almost all of those going on at the same time, which is a lot to carry on your plate. So I meet with them as a social worker to kind of talk about those barriers and what resources I can give them to help them with that and just kind of walk them through the steps. I don't like to do it all for them because I want them to learn how to do it themselves. Sometimes it does take a little bit extra.

And a lot of times it's just being there to listen to people because they haven't been able to talk to anybody. Nobody wants to hear it from them anymore. They've burned their bridges with everyone else and they just got a lot on their plate. And just to have someone to listen to everything can make a huge difference. Just to talk it out, just to have somebody listen. Yeah. So that's a big part of my job is just doing a lot of listening and identifying different resources that will help them. Just kind of linking them, helping them with the paperwork if they're having trouble understanding it, scanning and emailing it or faxing it for them cause they just don't have access to the internet or the skills to do it either.

Well, they learn how to make a resume. They learn how to do a mock interview. They do a lot of self-reflecting about things that they've done in the past and how they can improve that. Working on their self esteem is huge. A lot of people do not have a very high self esteem. Because they have never had a very good example and then they don't really know what to do. Then the abuse that they've suffered and all the other things pile onto it. Nobody's ever held them in really high regard. They don't see other people holding them as worthwhile, so they don't think they're worthwhile.

I just think it's amazing what the sisters and everyone has been able to do. Because it's so needed in Flint. There really aren't too many resources in this zone. Not a lot of people have transportation. They can come here, they can walk here and get everything, almost everything they need. I just think it's beautiful. It does feel like a big family here. And I get people coming in all the time that are like, I just from the moment I walked in the door, I just feel the love from this place and I never felt loved like that in my whole life. And that makes me want to cry cause that is so incredible.

I've had several people say "I was just walking by and something told me like to go inside. And then I've met everybody and it's just like changed my life. And I can't tell you how many people said that. The people that volunteer, the employees, we all get just as much out of this place as the people that come for services. You get so much out of like giving back and helping people.

It is pretty incredible when someone walks in the door and they tell us their story and then all of a sudden there's, you know, like five people just like, what can I get you? How about this? And you know, they probably are very overwhelmed at first. Like , you know, everywhere else I go, people treat me, you know, not very great. And then I come here and it's just like, they just feel that love instantly and I just think that's very special. And it's all free, which is really cool.

They feel like it's safe place in here for, you know, women or men to open up with me. And usually they are very open, surprisingly open. I feel like probably like 90% of the people that I meet with have been abused in some form in their life. It's really important that they know that there's places to go and resources and, um, counseling and all that for them if they choose..

We're constantly giving tours. There's always somebody who wants to check out the place and every time they are just so amazed at all the things that are happening in this building. They just all want to be a part of it and help out in some way once they see it. I want to try and do is see how to get more people just to come up and visit, just come up and visit. When they get the tour, just like, wow, I just really loved the way I feel when I'm in here. You know, there's something, there's an energy here.

Kapus Brown

[Kapus is an Army veteran who went through the men's program at the Center. He was later hired by Goyette Mechanical. He made a video for the Center while working to install copper pipes for Flint water. He also served on the Board of Directors]

When you go about a decade and some change and nothing never working out, no matter how good of attitudes you have, no matter how hard you try, you kinda get to a point where you start to begin to lose hope and think that things are just not going to work out for you. And what I can say is N.E.W Life did exactly what the name of the Center is. They gave me new life. In the sense of,

Kapus Brown

they gave me some hope. I started seeing light at the end of the tunnel and shed a lot of light on my darkness. That's what they did for me. N.E.W Life gave me a chance to do what I was good at, and they put me in contact with people to get my life moving in the right direction. I'm a plumber/pipefitter and I'm out here working on the water lines in my own city, I couldn't be happier.

Christine W.

My sister, Janie. Okay. She, um, tell me about the Center. How the people was nice. And she was telling me about the program. She was telling me about, you know, you have a career class, you have a sewing class. I'm like, I don't know about the sewing, but okay. I give it a try cause I never sewed before. So she told me about the program and that's when I called them asking like when do we start and stuff like that. I was really excited. The lady gave me a call back, telling me to come on up here and I been here ever since.

We bout to get ready and work in our resumes and um, they, um, helping us find, you know, about help us find employment and stuff like that. The people here are amazing. Everybody. It's like when you walk in the door, it's nothing but love in the air. Like it's, it's amazing how everybody is so nice and generous and the opportunities they can help you. Yesterday I volunteered and I was working in the food pantry and I loved it. I like it. I I'm like this where I want to work at. So yeah. So I found something that I really enjoy doing. So yeah. Sewing that ain't for me. I ain't doing that. Yeah. And I liked the food pantry because just looking at what they do and how they going into community and taking the food to the people. Old, elderly people. I thought that was amazing. Just to know that God helped with that. It makes me feel good. Yeah.

When a man told me to, um, put the food in a bag, like the potatoes, the onions and the oranges and the different stuff. I'm like, okay, I like that. And then he was telling me how many bags he needed so I was out on it, you know, doing it, everything. And then I liked to stock it. Like when you got to do the food boxes for the, the families and stuff, I really liked doing that. The canned goods and putting everything in a box, the cereal, the different stuff. He showed me one time and I was on it and he told me that I did an amazing job and stuff like that. You know, you're don't get too many compliments from people. So, you know, I was actually happy about it.

I graduated from high school. I did have goals and stuff like that. Things like I wanted to do, but then I put it on hold because here come my kids come along. So I put everything on hold, but at the same time, um, my mom wasn't there. You know, she wasn't in my life, but I thank God for my granny and my granddad. And you know, everybody else in my family, My mom had problems, she still do. She have a lot of problems where she gave me up when I was 6, but my granny took over and took care of me and my sister, my brother and my other sister. You know, it was four of us that she took care of. So I'm blessed to be where I'm at today.

My mother has drug issues where she's she put a man before kids? Like she's one of them type of women. She put a man before her kids and it's all about drugs. Like the drugs and stuff like that. She's not trying to get no help or anything, but all I know is

I wanted to be better than her. I wanted to take care of my kids. My kids not going to be in the system. If it didn't work out with their father, oh, well. I still wanted to take care of my kids and make sure they had the best. And um, I wanted to get them what I didn't have, you know?

Five kids, four boys and one girl. Yes, I did a pretty good job. Well, my daughter and my son's father, he's not in a picture because he sexual assaulted my daughter last year. She was 15 when it happened. I'm just glad he didn't take her innocence. And, uh, he was an okay person a long time ago. Cause you know, we dated in high school and stuff like that. Yes. I was like high school sweetheart type stuff. But at the same time, it was just when I was pregnant with my daughter, he was cheating on me. So I left him alone. I was just done. I couldn't deal with anymore. And as they got older, you know, um, I never thought in a million years that he would do something like this at all. But he did.

So he failed two polygraph tests. So yeah. So we're in a court process with that situation. We almost done, thank God we almost done. And my daughter is back to normal. She got her life back on track. She was doing good, you know, schools, everything she's doing really good. Okay, good. So, but we still have to go to court in May you see what I'm saying? So was just like at least everything else has been done but the trial. Yeah, the trial is coming up. Yes. Cause they trying to put the criminal case where his, uh, what's that word. They're going remove his parenting rights, you know, his rights of the children because I want his rights terminated period. Like I don't want him near my kids at all. And so, and everybody else has agreed saying the same thing. So we already know what's going to happen.

I dealt with that, but that was never the big issue. Cause that really wasn't the case why I came here. The reason why I came here because I was in a 10 year relationship with my two youngest, my 13 year old and my nine year old's father. That was mentally verbal, verbal abuse, just everything, just everything.

It was terrible. Like I tell anybody, if you have the chance to run, run. Like see the signs and just go. Cause that was the worst experience that I ever had to deal with. I never had to go through that with my daughter and my son's father or my 15 year old's father ever. I never had to deal with that with them guys, even though they wasn't okay, but they wasn't abusive or nothing like that. But my last two, their father, it took a toll on my life. The police is involved and I got to go get, uh, um, PPO to put out on him So he can't come over. You know, to protect us.

It went on, off and on for 10 years. In the beginning he was okay. Like he was okay. I didn't see no signs or anything just yet. But then it went from, I started noticing stuff, you know what I'm saying? Little stuff, that's coming up, missing out the house. Uh, some of the kids' stuff is coming up, missing at the house. Just being honest, like some of the kids' cell phones. I have had over 600 cell phones, literally 600 cell phones. I have receipts of every cell phone I ever, ever purchased. So because he used to sit up and ask me can he use my phone. And um, you know, I really don't like to share my phone. Not at all. I don't. So, but I was nice enough to let him see my phone. And he ended up selling my phone.

He ended up going to Metro again. That's what Metro first had came out and stuff like that. And that's when he ended up going there and getting my phone cut off and everything. And I'm like, what? Like, I didn't know, you can't actually do that to get somebody's phone cut off. But he did that. Well, now I know that he was on drugs. Know why? It's like, I felt like a lot of stuff. When I, once I was done, I started doing my research, asking questions and all types of stuff. But I found out that he was, um, cocaine. I found out he was on crack, pills. I don't know nothing about all these different pills, but he was on a lot of different stuff.

It can be where I always have friends, my friends, my family. I like to have get-togethers and stuff. You know, whatever I like to do, that's just me. I like to just have fun and enjoy family. And he didn't want my family around. He didn't want my friends around. It was like he had started an argument just so you can't do whatever you was going to do. Yeah. He'll start an argument. He'll get mad. He'll start, um, I had to call the police on him cause he had put holes in the wall. He broke my flat screen TV. He literally broke in one of my houses that I had a long time ago. Broke in the house and stole the kids' snacks, washing powder, my hot wings, and I love hot wings. It was just crazy. I'm like what is wrong with that dude?

But at the same time, it's like for one he was bipolar schizophrenia. And when you have that, you have to go to a doctor and you have to go get therapy. You have to be on meds, you know? And you have to let people know around you that you have that. I feel you supposed to so they can be aware. Let them, I didn't have the chance to make a decision if I wanted to deal with him or not, because it was like I'm forced. And then it got to the point when I tell him I don't want to be with him anymore. He had called me and get to saying, well, I'm about to kill myself. And you know, and that's scary. You know? Like I'm often to kill myself and you don't want to be with me. I'm going to kill myself. And I'm like, okay, we'll try to work then.

You know, feeling sorry for him. And then you okay for two, two weeks or three weeks. And then it goes back to the same thing over and over. And it just get worse and worse and worse. Where to the point where now my sons are involved. Every time something happened. I thank God for my other two kids' fathers that if anything, try to happen, whatever's going on. I let them know, come get the kids. And because they don't need to be over here to see this. So they did have my back on some things..

But at that time, before we found out where he is right now, he was a big help back then. Where if anything went on, he came, he was coming like, got the kids and stuff and everything. And he was very helpful. But you know, I don't understand why this man was like so jealous. Like I always had nice things, furniture, glass, I love glass. I think it's amazing to have glass. And he ended up, busting my glass table up that costed me like 800 bucks.

But it's just the whole point that this man didn't want to see me happy. He told me that my weight, talked about my weight. I have five kids. One kid died. My first child died of stillbirth, stillborn. So it was just like going through, you know, all of that. It was just a lot because you put me down, you mess with my self esteem. You finding any way to say, " No man gonna want to be with you, you got five kids." And you know, just saying all type of mean crazy things. And I told him, I'm not that type of woman. I go out here and live for anybody. Whoever God want me to be with, that's who I'm going to be with it. Might not be you. I'm just saying. So it was just like, it was to the point where I was just, I couldn't take it anymore. It was just stressing me out. My hair was falling out. It was a lot to see a person that say they love you, but you can't tell if they do or don't because how they act towards you. It was like, he hated me for no apparent reason because I put my kids before anything. And that you supposed to put your kids before anything, the bills and all of that stuff, but God, God always going to be first.

But at the same time, it was just like, he wanted me to put him first. He wanted me to listen to what he's talking about. Me, his expectations and all this other stuff. First of all, I'm not going to listen to you. Second of all, I got my own mind. And third of all, I thought I was paying all the bills and I'm doing it all. So I don't need you to tell me anything. And it starts with the arguments. He get mad. I had to sleep with a knife under my bed, my mattress for months at a time, because I didn't know what I was going to have to deal with that next day. You know, I'm waiting on people. I'm happy. I like to get up, get my kids off to school, turn my music on, play my music, make sure my house is clean. Cause I never know who's going to stop by. I got my food out because I'm cooking for dinner, you know and everything. And it's like, you starting an argument with me for no reason. " You is nothing. You ain't gonna never be nothing. That's why you ain't got no job and blah, blah, blah." I'm like, first of all, I don't have a job because my son have to, I have to take him back and forth to therapy and stuff, you know, or whatever, by him having a disability. So it's a reason why God put you where He want to put you right now. You want to work, but you can't work right now because this is what He wants you to do. And I can't get mad about that.

You know, this is my 17 year old, the oldest. Now I don't have to worry when I say he straight A's right now, straight A student. Back then? It was like he had a learning disability. He had speech impairment and some other stuff that they said, I can't really remember. Cause he'd been going to school ever since he was three, but I had a lot of people on my team that helped me through the process with him. And he's 17 years old. It's amazing. If something go wrong with your phone, ask him, he'll fix it. He knows how to he's very good at. Yeah. Yep. So I'm happy about that. And mind his own business, never gotten in trouble, never mess with no drugs or anything. So I am very blessed to have him, you know, I'm very blessed.

Him and my daughter, my daughter is 16 years old going to be 17. Majority of 16, 17s are having babies. Thank God she's, you know, doing what she supposed to do. And she got goals and, and she wants to talk to girls and you know, have a program where she can talk to girls and stuff like that about what happened to her. So they don't have to be silent anymore and they can talk about what happened to them and stuff like that. And I told her whatever she wanted to do, I'm there 100% to help her to get to wherever she want to go.

There was a lot of incidents, where one of them, he tried to kill himself at my house. A long time ago and I had to call his father and tell his father that he is going to commit, you know, kill himself. You know, he got a gun and everything. The last time he did that, he basically wanted to, I forgot. I had went somewhere. I was out with my friends, something, we went, we had went out or something and I came back home. I was so happy that I could have the chance to be out with my friends for once. I don't get that all the time. So that moment that I had, I enjoyed it. And it was like, I came home. It was like after two. And he started a whole argument with me and everything and literally said he had kill me and the kids ain't gonna have no mom.

And, and it was just crazy. Cause I wasn't expecting this, you know, I'm tired. I'd been dancing. I'd a got my money's worth. I'm dancing with everybody was just having fun. And it was just like that part. It hurt him because I didn't, I didn't understand like why is he doing this? Why are he doing these things to me? And then he wanted on people where if he mad at you, he want everybody else to be mad at you. Or he want to make everybody look at you like you're the bad person. Like you doing something to him. And I'm not doing anything to him. I'm not putting my hands on him. I don't put my hands on people. I'm not trying to go to jail. But for you to sit up here and threatened me.

I had a dog. Her name was Betty Boo. I loved Betty Boo. And he was jealous of my dog. Really jealous of her. And how you going, you gave me the dog. So I kept her. Cause I liked her. She got attached to me and the kids and named her. And one day I came home, he had my dog outside and it was freezing cold. And I'm like, she's a house dog. She not going to be outside. She's a house dog. And, and I said, I said, "Baby, I wish y'all could talk to me to tell me." Cause she, her leg was, she was limping. She wasn't limping before. So apparently he was messing with her, you know, messed her leg up. I don't know what he did to her. But after that day she was real scared and furious. Like she would not go by him or anything. He hurt the dog. Yeah. And she was just, I was like crying for her because I'm like, I wish you can talk to me and tell me something. So I took her to the vet and whoo they expensive. And that's when they said that somebody had to pull her, um, her leg out of place, something like that. They tried to explain to me. They wrapped it or whatever. And she was okay. I think they said out of place. So yes. I'm like, yeah. And um, you know, so she was okay.

My son that's 13 now, he had basically set the house on fire in the basement. But yeah, he was only 5 going on 6 years old. That's when I found out years ago that he was bipolar schizophrenic, but I got him help though. You know what I'm saying? I got them helping everything. And um, they daddy knew that the house was on fire. You know, it was bad, bad, but it wasn't where you can't live there. And my landlord was so amazing. He had his workers to come out, redid my basement, helped me get whatever I needed for the house though. It was amazing. So I was very blessed. I love that man to this day.

It was just completely done after that. After the house got caught on fire and stuff, we came home. I was staying with my sister for a little bit and to, they got the stuff out the basement, cause that smell was still down there and he was there and um, it was me, Malakai and my other son. Cause we gonna go home and y'all said y'all wanted to help me clean. So that's what we gonna do. And so when we got there day, their dad was already there. Cause he kept calling my phone. Like where did you go? And I'm like, why? You know what I'm saying? Like, why are you calling me? So we got there. He basically was just starting an argument and I'm already cleaning and stuff. I got, majority of everything had done. So I actually happy about that. So we took the bags out, put them on a curb.

And um, that's when he came, he came in, was like, you ain't answer y'all phone and all this other stuff. And I said, I'm not answering my phone because right now I got the music on. You can't hear. And we trying to get this done before the people come the next day to do the paint and do everything they got to do. And he came in with gasoline and he was just basically started a whole argument with me for no apparent reason and was like," I'm gonna take the boys from you and they ain't gonna have no mom, I'll finish you, set you on fire" and all this other stuff. And my son at the time Marquell, he's 13 now. But at the time he was 10, 11, somewhere like that. And Marquell ended up running next door, running next door to my neighbor's house and telling her to, can I call the police? My dad was trying to kill my mom, trying to kill my mom and everything. He got gasoline and stuff.

My Malaki he standing in the door at the time. Malaki is real young and he done just peed on his stuff because he's terrified. He's scared. So now I got to figure out how I'm going to get myself, cause I'm, how my mind is thinking. I'm a kill you before you kill me. This is how my mind is. Cause I'm like, I'm not going to let you kill me. All my kids needs me. And that's when, um, the police had pulled up and everything. Oh, they came, they came real deep. And so they came, he got arrested and stuff like that. And they basically told him that by him having gasoline in my house, in my home, they can charge him with, um, they can charge him with attempted murder. Yeah they can charge him with attempted murder and stuff like that. And they asked me that I want to press charges. I said, yes, I did everything they asked me to do. So I thank God that Flint police came. I went and got a PPO out on him. And after that, I really didn't have to deal with him anymore.

I went to Georgia because I wanted a better life for me and my kids. Not just that, to get away from everybody, family, just everybody. I just needed to get away. But it was just, I was getting threatened every year. I was scared to even check my voicemail. Every year for 5 years, this man have called me and threatened me. And so every time he called, I tell him that you can't talk to the kids until you get your life together. Because the last conversation you had with the boys, he was basically saying like, yeah, disrespect your mom. And then my son, he just hung up. Cause he was like, I don't want to hear that. You know, these are young kids, we talking about and the kids was in therapy and stuff like that. I dealt with that for 5 years. So when things didn't go his way, he would call and be like, I'm gonna have somebody to do something to you and this and that. And you're going to die and all of this other stuff. I deal with that for 5 years on my own. And I got to the point, I stopped checking my voicemail. I guess I have to change my number.

So the reason why I came back because my granny got cancer. Otherwise I woulda stayed in Georgia. Yeah. So I had to, because she was calling me back to back like. They telling me that she inna hospital, Thanksgiving and Christmas. I'm like, okay, I can't do this. Cause if something happened to my granny, I'm gonna lose it. Like I gots to be here. So I stopped everything to come back here.

After this program? Working. I met a lot of people and still communicate with everybody in the program and the people around here that I met when I grew a relationship with everybody. So it was just like at the same time I liked being here. And one of my goals are to, I would like to open up my own shelter for women, children, and men, because it's men out there that got custody of their kids and they need help too. Cause they don't get a lot of resources like women get. So I want to be able to help them. And that's why cause I seen the light in Georgia by all these people got all this money and then nobody doing nothing. But at the same time they ain't got that many shelters here either. And the [shelters] giving these people the run around, run around on getting help and this and that.

I want to make sure I get the people the right information. And that was my whole goal to open up my own shelter for women, children, and men. Help them as much as I can. I might not be able to help everybody, but I want to help somebody and to talk to women, to tell them my story and what I went through, because it is hard to get out of a relationship and go on because you feel like you can't do it without that person, but actually you can. So it took me 5 years to build my confidence, my self-esteem up. You can't stop me now. I'm where I need to be. So I'm happy with that. I want to work here. When I did the food pantry, I'm like, I like this. This is where I, you know, this is where I want to be. Cause I like helping people. If they can't hire me, I still would come back and volunteer. I'd do that anyway.

I'm learning. Yeah. Putting me first for once. The kids is getting older and I just want to show them that, you know, I'm doing this for them and myself. And I want a job. So when my kids go to school or whatever, they be like, "my mom at work," and stuff like that. So I've been in three car accidents. I survived all three, I was not the one that was driving, but the people that I was with. I want to get over my fear and I want to learn how to drive. Cause I want my own truck, car, whatever it may be. And I want to get up and say, Oh, we off, we go today.

They helped me a whole lot. And I thank, and I thank them so much because they say you can talk about anything. Some places don't even let you talk about anything. It just brung us even closer because you, your situation might think bad. Her situation might think bad, but everybody came together. So it ain't a point of pointing fingers at nobody because everybody went through something and it's the point that we overcame it. And the plan was we came in here together, we gonna leave together. So it's amazing being here. It's amazing being around lovable people. It's amazing how I see the stuff that they do for the community. That's amazing. You know? So I love being in this program.

I just hope it can help somebody else. And you know, and to get it out there that there is help here. And a lot of women be feeling like they can't, you can, it ain't even no such word as can't. You can, you can do whatever you put your mind to. And I have been through a lot, you know, first they daddy, first, my son. Right now, he's 13 and in a juvenile facility because him and some boys robbed a pizza guy with a BB gun. So it's like, it's only so much you can do as a parent. I'm not going to blame myself because I told you right from wrong, what to do, what not to do. And if you want to follow in your father's footsteps, then that's something you're going to have to live with. Because I can't, I can't tell you how to live your life. I got 14 days to move because of what my son did.....

Nicole Zepp

I am currently one of the seamstresses and I am machine maintenance in the sewing. I have seven and a half years of sobriety. I started coming to the center six, uh, seven years ago

Supervisor Cathy Oostermeyer and Nicole Zepp work out a new Stormy Kromer vest

this week through New Path[s]. I was in the recovery program. I was not in their alternative to incarceration program. I grew up as a Navy brat. Literally. I needed that [military] structure. I had some very t r a u m a t i c c h i l d h o o d experiences that led me to drink a very young age. I started drinking at age nine.

I had 30 years. Not always drinking. I had some dry time during that, but 30 years before I became sober, approximately 30 years before I became sober . I didn't really, I don't believe I hit my rock bottom until six months after I stopped, uh, using my secondary drug of choice. My primary was alcohol and my [drug] was benzodiazepans. Which is Xanax out of N Klonopin. And during that time I signed my rights away to my four children. During my active addiction I also had a very abusive marriage and a lot of other things that go with being in abusive relationships.

Uh, when I came to the center, I couldn't raise my head, let alone have the sisters look at me without bawling. I went to the Genesee Access Center and they referred me to New Path. We have at St Luke's we have actually a program, um, that we run once a week for the ladies from New Path. They come here once a week and they have a book called 40 Day Lovefest that they read and it teaches them basically how to love themselves.

I was part of the first employment prep program we had. That was February of 2013. I've been working for the Center since May 6th of 2013. So in February I started the employment preparation programs. Back then it was only 15 hours of volunteer work. I had already, probably within three weeks I had accumulated that. I had already been volunteering when St Mike's had their breakfast program. I'd already been volunteering with them.

I was volunteering at the Center once I started the work program, I was at the Center three days a week. After I graduated from that work program, I was right into full-time employment here at the Center of sewing. Yes. I'm on the Stormy Kromer line. I have done the swim dresses. I've sown with both of the Tracy Reese lines we've done. When we were doing the scrubs, I was primary cutter.

It's a safe place, but not what I'm looking for right now. If I get a raise, I'm going to lose my Medicaid. And with my health issues, I need the health benefits. And the Center can't pay benefits. I've been through family crisis. The sisters have been supportive. I've reconnected with my children. Three of my four children I reconnected with while I've been here. Last year my brother became a double amputee. And the Center had been very supportive of me.

I was sent to New Path, 11 months. Legit. I tell a lot of people I wanted to move out of New Path in July. I wanted to leave. Sister Carol knew I wasn't ready to leave. She grounded me to New Path. She put it September 15th. I left September 3rd. Okay. So she grounded me. Catholic guilt. If I would've left in July, I wouldn't have made it.

Annette Rowe

I've always volunteered wherever my kids were. St Robert's and then Powers. And so, okay, its 2010 and my son's kind of going on. What do I do next? I was looking for a place to volunteer. And Dave Wolbert said to us at a downtown dinner, "I have this place that you should come to. It's Durant Tuuri Mott, Come in the afternoons and you could mentor and tutor kids. I wasn't really sold on it, but I thought, okay, let's try it out. But the next day Steve Wolbert [Dave's son] calls and says, " Wait, Mrs. Rowe, I have a better idea. Come to St. Luke's. This is perfect. And by the way, I made an appointment for you at 11 o'clock to meet Sister Carol." And I'm like, what? I couldn't back out. I had an appointment.

So I walked in the door and Sister wanted me to go to the literacy program. I'm like, ain't going to happen because I'm not, I'm not teacher material. So she put Sister Rita in charge of me. Sister Rita at the time did the New Paths women who were there as an alternative to incarceration. Right? And so my joke was, "What you do at Luke's? Whatever Sister Rita tells you to."

So I would come in every Wednesday and mentor them. You look people in the eye and you tell them, "I believe in you." Every week it's a different group and a different story. It breaks your heart. So I call St Luke's my moral compass. It teaches me how to be. It teaches me that when I get a hangnail, suck it up. You don't have anything to complain about. Yeah. And I get more out of this than I give. And Sister Carol, you want to be just like her when you grow up, don't you? Yeah, God will provide. She just makes it all seem so easy.

But I tell the girls when I'm here, even if I'm not here my mind is still here and I'm always trying to determin what can we do for them? You listen a lot and you believe in them because the girls I deal with, their stories are just inconceivable. The people that I've worked with, we've worked with here are second and third generation that nobody's talking about. But if we could come into this town and just help one person, that's what you need. If you could just reach out to one, affect one person for the better. You know, if you're out somewhere, you tell people, all they have to do is walk in the door. That's all you have to do is walk in the door and you get it. And so that's what you have to do is get people in the door.

We have a schedule on the wall for the New Paths women. 9 to 10 it's exercise and Bible study at 10 to 11 it's crocheting, 11 to 12 it's usually the 40 Days To Happiness or some kind of class. 12 o'clock we eat. One o'clock we usually have another class and two o'clock another class. Sometimes it's jewelry making or sometimes we'll watch a movie. Or if sister doesn't have anything, she'll look at me and go, "Can you do your dental hygiene lecture?" So I do dental hygiene, nutrition lecture. I always carry my stuff just in case I need to pull a rabbit out of my hat.

Tiffany DePriest-McIntyre

I had dropped out in 1995 and you know, a couple of things. Dropped out of 9th grade. I was a young student and I was a young mother. I just had a child and I also got bit by a spider and it had kind of messed up my legs. I was going to lose my shins. So, I had to drop out because I couldn't go to school and take care of my baby and take care of myself.

That was in Kenosha, Wisconsin. I was following my brother. I think he got out of Job Corps and he went through a lot of trades and he didn't want to leave me behind, so he wanted me to come follow him around. We are really close. We started in Toledo, Ohio and we ended up in Kenosha, Wisconsin because there was a job that he was looking into in landscaping and building houses and everything. So I ended up going to school there. It was just a lot for a teenager. I was a young 14-15 year old student and a mother too.

I had moved [to Flint] and I was going through a 4-year stage of depression, major depression, bipolar, all of that type of creepy stuff. And I moved back home. My son was kind of sick so I moved closer to him so I could be close without having to travel because I was in Saginaw when I went into the depression. So, I moved back, and I stayed about a block and a half away and I was coming to a food drive [at the Center] and the ladies introduced me to the women's group. It is a group of women getting together on Wednesdays. I thought it was awesome. I got to know a lot of people and everything and I wanted to be more involved in the community as I was coming back to life.

They have a group, it is a couple of sisters, well ladies, they are not Catholic nuns. They [the women] get together and they pray, they exercise, eat, do crafts and everything. We watch movies. It goes from 9-3 and I thought it was very interesting, you know praying and just bonding and telling your stories, sharing and everybody lend an ear and shoulder. I thought that was awesome and as I got comfortable, I wanted to become more involved so I asked around to see if there is anything that I could help, in any way. Sister Carol brought me down to this basement and, if I could just show you how it was when I first walked down you would be at an awe, like, oh my. It was a disaster. You walk in, that is all you could do is walk in. There were bags and boxes everywhere. It just wasn't organized.

There was a lot of stuff. Household needs, personals, shoes, clothing, all types of stuff. I am an organizer, so she brought me down here and I just started organizing things. I came here 7 months ago. It was about March or April. Sister Carol brought me down here [to the basement] and I have been down here ever since.

I then joined the job program. I joined the literacy program so I could continue my education. The job program that will get you in motion of learning trades and skills and everything, budgeting. It is a 16-week program. I graduated the end of August. And I was also asked to mentor this next class. It will be back and forth, if they need me, they will let me know. Because I try to keep this going so I can keep helping the community, you know, less stress on the Sisters. That is pretty much what I do.

Tiffany DePriest-McIntyre

As they come in, I sort all of the donations and put them out. People just bring in bags and boxes and crates and luggage, however it come in and from the office. They sort through them and send them to whatever department they need to go to, linens, fabrics, baby, furniture and then I get the rest of it. I sort it out on Tuesday, and Thursdays I will have it up for the community on the racks and tables. And people can just come in and take whatever they need. No questions, no price, no cost. Everything is free. Nine times out of 10, they come during the food drive, on Tuesday and Thursdays from 10-2. I just make sure that there is a lot out there so they can have things they can look through and shop for.

I am actually here Monday through Friday. I volunteer on Monday then Tuesday, Wednesday and Thursday I am an employee and on Friday I volunteer as well. When I volunteer, I do the same thing, like I am on the clock. I pretty much do the same thing. Now I am working on my GED. It's like starting all the way over because that is pretty much the way I had to go. Start all the way over. Which is fine I set a goal date for next year. June or July. Hopefully I make it.

Oh, I love it here. This is such a wonderful place. I introduce everyone to this place because, it is great here. Everybody here is lovable and they welcome. They have a lot to offer. Especially if you are headed in the wrong direction. I was going through depression, but I could see people coming in from on the streets, off the streets, homeless, on drugs, off drugs, it doesn't matter. Whomever come in the door, they get comfortable. It is like a family. Which is awesome. It brought me to tears. I walked in and everybody believe. I was like "oh man, I got to go home!" [I'm so overwhelmed] This is an awesome place and they have a lot to offer. A lot of trades and everything. I learn a lot here. Even if, I feel like I have fallen off the earth. You know I will be 41 in November, but that depression stage sent me to like, I didn't have no one and nobody cared for me. And once I was introduced to this place, it woke me up. They are really lovable.

Rachel H.

I believe that our life goes in cycles, like how the seasons are. So like in spring God is usually starting something new. In the summer, we work hard towards it. And then in the fall we produce a harvest from that. And then in the winter we reflect on that thing. So it was coming towards, I believe, January and I was asking God what he was having for me for the spring coming up. And I was led to a Bible study led by a nun. I'm not real sure on the location, but it was on the north end. It was a place that was like a kitchen where you can go every day, a couple of days a week and get something to eat.

I started going there to get food and to eat. One of the girls invited me, she said, Oh, on Wednesday mornings they have a Bible study that the nun holds, across the street. So then I started going to Bible study there. I've been a Christian since 2000, but it's new to me to study the Bible. But I always like an opportunity. I did feel like I said that God was leading me there. And then after a few weeks of going there, then [St Luke's] got brought up. I felt very strongly about attending. And I said, I think that God's opening this door for me in my life. I've been married several times in my life. I've worked off and on, but I've mostly been financially dependent upon the men that I've been with. I've lived middle-class.

I got divorced and ended up living here [in Flint]. And so this is the first time I've ever lived in an inner city in my life. So it's been very different for me because I've had to adapt just from the cultural differences. The way that I act is how you acted to survive in a middle-class society. And a lot of it is very different than how you are and how you act in, I don't know, what do they even call it? Maybe in the ghetto, in poverty. I, you know what I'm saying? I had to learn, I'm learning the hard way, you know, that I'm saying things that are offensive or the way that I'm acting. And it's been 10 years and it's just who I am.

I went from one man to another man to survive. So I've been with that man since pretty much six months after the divorce. I just put myself back in very similar situation. As we're learning from the YWCA, there's different forms of abuse. So it's, uh, it's financial control. So, you know, limiting my choices or getting me to self-sabotage myself when financial opportunities arise. Cause that results in, that could result in independence. Right. You know, and I always say, well, do you want me to stay because I love you or do you want me to stay because you forced me, manipulated me to stay. Are you so afraid that if I have a choice that I'm not going to choose to stay. I've been very direct about it. You're trapped. You can't leave. And then there's also social isolation that you're not free to associate with whom you want or do what you want to do.

I'm not gonna scream victim mentality. I play an equal role because you allow things to happen on some levels. So, you have to come to a state where you're willing to acknowledge your responsibility and your parts in it and the things you allow. I've come to the place where I can say, okay, I think I'm ready this time. [The N.E.W. Life Center] is providing me the support and the services that I need. I feel like the girls, we pray for each other. So there's some spiritual support. Their [the Center's] mission and their goal obviously is to reflect the love of Christ and to bring the gospel to life and to do what Christ has commanded them to. They're just being obedient. Then it's up to God and the Holy Spirit.

Tim Goyette

I have been here for about 5 years now. My oldest son, Richard, is a very good friend of Steve Wolbert and I was going through, kind of a dark period of my life, frankly, for a couple different reasons and my son, who was pretty into it of how I am feeling, suggested that I meet with Steve. We have both known Steve for a long time, but he said, "I think you should meet with Steve because he does a lot of work for this group on the north-end of town and I think you would be interested" I thought, well that's weird but ok I will call Steve, We ended up having lunch at the deli downtown and consequently, Steve said "Tim, I really think you should come see what we are doing at St. Luke's, I think it is right up your alley because you have some business experience plus you are kind of a spiritual guy and we are also looking for someone, frankly, to get involved in our men's program. We want to make some changes in that." I said, "okay, I will come." I was just taken aback the very first time I saw it, which I am sure it is a pretty familiar...

It's certainly not the physical appearance of the place. I was driving here thinking "what in the world am I getting into?" you know, but anyways, I was taken aback by the Sisters at first, about just their love for people, kind of unconditional love but just that, and the other thing that stood out to me was their commitment to try to empower people to better themselves, not just to be a place to get a handout. That really resonated with me. Um, so from there, I got involved in the men's program and the whole thing about trying to get, particularly the men, kind of restarted on their lives, if you will, second chance, third chance, and get them into the work force.

I talked to the Sisters about when I first came here, as to what I could do to help the men's program. The other thing Sister Judy recognized was when we had talked a little bit, she said "so, you are an ex-teacher?" and I had been in a whole other life, I was a teacher, taught secondary education and she said, "ok, this could be a good fit for you!" So, Sister Judy and I were kindred spirits in that respect.

The men come once a day 9am to 3pm for 16 weeks and then another day they come in to do volunteer hours. When they complete the program, pass a drug test, get their volunteer hours in and attend class regularly, they get to graduate. We talk about a lot of things, about self-confidence, about trying to figure out what we have tried in the past that doesn't work. So we will need to try something new. Meaning, lots of different things. We could, kind of look at liking it to when Jesus said, "You know you need to build on rock rather than sand." What that means to us and, then of course our message to them are things like getting your GED; getting your driver's license; cleaning up your criminal record; getting more in touch with God; and doing the right things.

Those are all thing that will start building upon and from there we can start getting your life better and your family's life better, than all of these things that we have been putting off, if you know what I mean. Rather than just saying "well I don't have my GED, but I am going to get a job anyway." That usually leads to, as work slows down, you are let go or you are not able to advance in that position because you don't have a GED. That is just one example of the things that we try to say. We need to take where you are at right now, let you know that we believe in you, we want to be here for you, we want to help guide you through the steps that you need to improve your life.

Each one in the class has personal issues, reasons? There

are guys that have abuse issues, mental issues, homeless issues, economic self-esteem issues. We try to meet them right where they are at, and try to find out do you need counseling? What do you need to do in order to get your driver's license? Do you need to start going to GED classes and get your GED?" Those are all things that we try to identify with them and let them know hey, we are on your team. We can be your cheerleaders. But at the end of the day, you have to do it too. You have to be the guy that is driving this bus. We will help you out but, we can't do it for you, you have to do it.

Early days of the men's lawncare program

Passion for the Mission

- **Focus On Programs, Social Enterprises, Food Pantry, Literacy**

- **Have a Non-Judgmental Attitude**

- **Use your God-Given Inner Drive For the Good of Others**

- **Give All You Can To the Mission**

DOROTHEA GUICE

I got on disability and I couldn't work for about a couple of years or so. Without work and dealing with my physical issues and as I was going to doctors and therapists then my body was straightened in the back. I was ready to go back to work. And we had a family friend that was working here and she was on disability. So I was trying to find a company that recognizes disabilities. And so she led me here. I went through the training program. It was wonderful. It made you realize that this is kind of where I needed to be because of the spiritual awareness and the helping, you know, all the help they did in the community. The understanding that I received and then especially kind of the one that is the special part of the program is dealing with your emotional issues. Um, and it was a change for me because I had never been out of work. And so to be out of work due to a physical disability was kind of hard on me. So to try to accept what it was and move forward.

After graduation we had to still volunteer for about two more years. When you're a volunteer we help do Teddy bears and we were sorting fabrics and sewing dog collar guards at the time. I was still coming to the women's group on Wednesdays. Just giving me something to do outside of the house, keeping me moving. And so after that, that's when they had got the bear order and they needed some help with the bears to complete the bears on the time frame that he was supposed to be completed. So that's when Sister Carol called us and asked us if we wanted to volunteer to help do the bears. We were still volunteering, proving ourselves.

I sewed some clothes at home and took the best ones to show Sister Carol what I could do. And when she saw the kind of work that I could do she did tell us that we will be hired before the next year. I've been here for four years. They had two sides when we came here, the special projects and Stormy Kromer side. So when you first came in, you were on the special projects side to, you know, increase your sewing abilities and just see what kind of skills you had in order to be moved over to the Stormy Kromer side.

During the Flint water crisis, Mel [Chin, an artist] and Tracy [Reese, fashion designer] had a found out about the Center and the clothes we were making. Mel had [art exhibits] in New York. Tracy Reese is a Detroit fashion designer. And Flint Fit was involved. They met at the Center and came up with the idea to

Photo courtesy Queens Museum_Mel Chin

make clothing out of recycled water bottle fabric. After we finished up the project Mel and Tracy was giving a fashion show in New York on our clothes. They put names in the hat and I was one of the 3 that got to go to New York City.

So, and it was awesome to be in a fashion show in New York. It was for us to watch our products that we made at a fashion show at the Queens Museum. And it was, it was awesome. Everything that all of us made was in the fashion show, the caps, hats, bras and skirts. [And we're doing raincoats now and tote bags]

They flew us out to New York. Yeah, they paid for the hotel stay. [It was] right before the Manhattan bridge. When you looked out at night you could just see the bridge and everything. So, um, and it was a really nice hotel that we stayed here. Where we were staying it was like all types of things up and down the street, you know, restaurants and jazz clubs and stuff like that. When we first got there, we just went exploring, you know. We just like, we just going to go exploring. We rode the subway everywhere. I was like, I need to experience this. We went to Brooklyn. We went to that tattoo, wig shop that's supposed to be so big on TV. We just rolled until we just got so tired we had to go in. I bought everybody a souvenir with $80 that was given to me. Okay. I spent it on the ladies here in sewing. New York key chains and New York pins.

The next day everything was tied down with the fashion show. you know, getting ready and going to rehearsals and everything like that. I really enjoyed it. The fashion show was at the Queens Museum. I'm not sure exactly where it is. It was all about positivity, no matter, you know, the negative that we experience with the lot of issues. They took that negative and made it a positive and it was all about what does water mean to you. How you can take a tragedy and make out it of a positive thing that moves forward and something that you can basically kind of progress with. They had a positive motivated speaker. Everything was positive in spite of the negative that, you know, we experienced here.

It was packed. There must have been a thousand people there. I mean it brought tears to the eyes of the audience, you know. And it was very emotional. We walked down the runway with our model. As we were walking, they had our voices, we had sent a recording on what water means to us. And so they had our voices playing as we met our models [as they came] down the spiral stairs and we walked with them down the runway. After it was over they called Mel and Tracy for recognition. They give them recognition of putting this together. Tracy cried. The crowd was just, like they're crying. I was crying. It was awesome.

STEVE WOLBERT

I was working at St. John Vianney for Fr. Tom Firestone who hired me as the director of development. I got into fundraising and figuring out how the school could remain open. Fr. Tom said to go out [to the St Luke N.E.W. Life Center] and meet with these two nuns and see if there is a way that you can help them. They're doing something kind of cool. And so I went there and started talking to the sisters about fundraising. And, I mean, it's like you walk in there and you meet the sisters and you're just like, there is something about this place.

They had, I think, just started or they might have had three or four or five part-time women working in the sewing business. It was a really small kind of like thing that they were doing. They had the three-year program of Life Change. Every Wednesday for three years the women had to show up. And it's clearly evolved since that time of having a handful of women that were working there. I would have been getting involved out there just as the Center was going through the hard time of transitioning from that three-year program where women were able to get the entry level jobs to when the economy kind of evaporated. I remember Sister Carol, Sister Judy talking about-- they had to decide if they wanted to stick with their dream and the thing that they had prayed about, the mission about helping women become self-sustainable or did they want to become like this kind of job preparation program. And so that's why they started the sewing business as a way to employ the women after that had graduated from the program.

And I really didn't get really involved though until 2012 when we started the Alternative Spring Break Program. Fr. Tom, my dad and the sisters started bringing college students to Flint. Every Sunday they would meet Fr. Tom. Every Monday night they would meet the sisters. On Tuesday they would go out to St. Lukes. And so I got to know the sisters and hear their story on a more regular basis.

I'll never forget one day that really sold me out there. It was Virginia Tech students that were here for Alternative Spring Break. They were installing the first dropped ceiling in the cafeteria. So all the dropped ceilings at St. Lukes were done by college students. Every year they'd do a room. And so this was the first year and it was our first time doing the program in Flint. They were out there on I think like Thursday. And they got it probably, you know, a little over halfway done. But they did the hard stuff. They got it framed out and they had a volunteer there who was showing them how to do it and he was going to finish the job.

They had finished their service and they were supposed to have a free afternoon on Friday. They said no, we want to go back to St. Lukes and finish that ceiling. And they got to the point where they had one tile left. And so these are, you know, 16 college students. They had one tile left. Looking back on it, if I'm one of those college students, I'd probably say, hell yeah, I want to be the person that puts this last ceiling tile in. But they went and they grabbed Sister Carol and they had her put the ceiling tile in. And Sister Carol, I will never forget, when she put that tile in and she kind of like turned around with a look of pure joy on her face from this very simple thing. I mean she's doing these monumental life changing things on a regular basis for people. "But for those students to have Sister Carol be the one to put in the last tile..." was like a moment that kind of hooked me out there forever.

I tend to get stuck with stuff after the sisters do it. It's kind of how it happens. So Sister Judy will have a dream. Sister Carol and Sister Judy will make it happen. And then, you know, ninety days later I will show up out there and there will be like a hoop house on the property built operational with the stuff growing. And it's just like when did that happen? And they just kind of look at you and say all right. I mean, you know, I may have played a role on seeing some of that stuff [like the men's programs] move along. But I mean the sisters were going to make it happen anyway. I just kind of like was able to connect a couple of dots or find some sources that they might not have had.

I mean the way I always look at it is like can you believe we get to be a part of something like this? I think the thing that's really unique out there and what I hope the people who, you know, would give me credit for being out there would talk about is how like, you know, I have been lucky enough to get to build a personal relationship with the sisters and kind of get the cure. And I remember it must have been the beer talking that gave me this like moment of zen when I realized that, you know, the sisters care as much about the Steve Wolberts of the world who are going there without these like major problems on paper and, you know, having these challenged up-bringings. There is as much there for me to have an experience at St. Lukes as it is for the men and women that go through the program.

It's just like, "No sisters, thank you for having this place."

It was like five years ago I remember walking into the Board meeting in February and being blindsided that every person was being laid off at the Center. It was just like your heart gets ripped out of your chest. The sisters had to talk to the men and women on their own. I just felt like absolute dirt. I thought that SIPI [Social Impact Philanthropy Investment, Steve's company] should try to help out. And so we had a proposal at the March board meeting and SIPI started working there that month. And that was our first contract. I think that we've grown together, you know, as we figured out who we are as a company and the services that we offer. I think you can also see like a line to where St. Lukes has grown and become more organized.

I've staffed a few of the missions at Masses in other parishes. I was sitting back and, you know, selling cookies after Mass. I have been to so many of them at this point that you just, you can spot the people who you know are just going to be like, they're going to cave for the sisters. And I'll never forget one of them. Sister Carol is just talking to this guy. And this is a big, you know, 6'2" older guy and he's talking to Sister Carol. Next thing I look over he's kind of like wiping his eyes. And I'm just sitting there like oh my gosh. This poor guy he's getting hooked. You know, she's just being herself. There is no demand. There is no guilt trip. Nobody is doing any of that. It's just that they tell the story and if you would help they'd be so grateful.

JOE PARKS

I retired from the Sheriff's Department as a detective, in 2012. Then I shot all of the deer, caught all of the fish and I was looking for something to do other than that. I volunteered a little bit in '14 and '15 [at the Center] and was working with the men's class. They had a lot of volunteers that showed up to help with that and I didn't want to be at a place that had too many volunteers. So, I moved to security. Then they got me working in the pantry. I had found out about St Luke's from Tim Goyette, he's my brother-in-law. He tried to get me to come here for 6 months and when I did I just fell in love with the nuns. They have it figured out. They just got it figured out. For 35 years with the Sheriff's Department I had thought put the bad guy in jail, life is good. And then I came here.

Joe Parks
Food Distribution
Day

I work with the pantry. I have a good influence with the Food Bank now, so I was able to get a lot more food for a lot less money. Since we got that yellow truck out there, I filled that up yesterday for $50, it usually costs up $1200. A big difference. I didn't get meat or canned goods. Those are the expensive things. But we are trying to use our extra stuff. We haven't had a bill from the Food Bank in a month now. We get food from McLaren Hospital. I am working on getting food from Genesys Hospital. I am working on all of the thrift stores around here, to give us free bread. Gordon Foods, they take care of us really well at Christmas. And now I am working on Sam's Club and Meijer to donate food.

We distribute food here 2 days a week. Once a month 3 days a week. Volunteers sign up people as they come in. And the size of the family dictates the size of the food. It is kind of a three-step process. They go through Josephine with their files; they come over here and they are re-registered to make sure they have the proper number of people and they also sign up for Christmas. Then they tell us how many in each family. We try to prepare the bags the day before, so as soon as the number comes out, we just put it on the cart. A 1, 2 [persons], we call it a single bag, a 3, 4 and 5, 6 and up, are all the same. But, because we know who is homeless, it dictates what we give them. Like, giving them a bag of meat isn't going to do them any good because they have no place to cook it. But we have been saving our canned meat and we just recently got a donation from a lady I know, her mother passed away and she was a hoarder and she thought the world was going to end. So, she had $25,000 worth of freeze-dried food, like camping food. All you have to do is add hot water and I have been distributing that to the homeless and most just use cold water and they say, "it is not restaurant quality, but it is better than starving."

The bags we give out depending on how many is in the family, there is canned goods, there is rice, cereals, breads, sweets. Um, depending on if we have them, there will be eggs, milk, macaroni and cheese, spaghetti noodles. Depending on how many they have in the family is how many they get. They all get the basic things and then on top of that, they get all of the fresh produce that we get from the Food Bank.

And the Food Bank has been very generous and for the last 6-weeks, gave us an extra truck full of food for free, every week. We just put the crates in the parking lot, and they can take all they want. And all they have to do is pull up, in the parking lot, and we will give them food. We don't pay for any of that food. Anything getting past fresh, we stick it out there and people can just take it. Those split peas outside came from Our Lady of Guadalupe. One of the guys from the pantry at Our Lady of Guadalupe has a hog farm, so we call him when our carrots are going bad and he brings us food and takes the carrots to feed the pigs. And then he will slaughter a pig and give us one!

We are trying to get partnerships with Our Lady of Guadalupe, St. Mary's on the east side, the Warming Center. So, if somebody has too much of the same thing, we can work something out. It usually costs $5-6,000 a month to run the pantry. Well, we take care of the ones we know need to be taken care of. Thank goodness we took care of that lady today. We just added a new thing, we deliver food now. Some of them just can't make it here and they shouldn't.

This place, it is unbelievable that this place never gets damaged. It is like a sanctuary it really is. Everyone is showed love, respect and dignity. What I have learned, with people, is they just want to be listened to. I might go in there and have a girl crying for 15-20 minutes. You just listen to them. Like I said, you go 20 minutes with a lady crying and not say a word and she hugs you and says, "thank you", and you didn't even say anything.

I take probably, once every two weeks, maybe once a week, a woman down to the shelter because of domestic violence. Down at the YWCA. And we will get them booked into the Y. Go home, get their clothes, get their kids. And be safe for a while.

Cathy Oostermeyer

I have been the sewing supervisor since February 2018. It all started before that because I wanted to put my daughters through Powers High School. At the time, I was a stay at home mom. My daughter's graduated now, but at the time, I said "okay, I am going back to work. I am going to look for a job and everything" so, I was talking with Father Paul Schwermer.

And, um, right about that same time, you know he was going through his last stages, so, his melanoma cancer, at the same time Mary, who has also passed away from cancer, at St. Roberts, one of the secretaries there, handed me a piece of paper and it was a job opening at St. Charles & Helena for secretary and bulletin editor. I was so excited about that and I told Father Paul and he's like "this is for you." I think he had something to do with it because a couple days after that he passed away I got a phone call, like two days after, to come in for an interview, so, it was all connected.

So I went there and worked part-time for Father Ken Coughlin for almost three years and, as I am working on my bulletins, I look at other bulletins, you know, to get ideas to see if I am on the right track and don't need to reinvent the wheel, so, and then I came across this job opening, it said "Sewing Supervisor" and I am like, "hmm, what is that about?" The ad was in the St Matt's bulletin and it was for St. Luke's N.E.W. Life Center. They needed a sewing supervisor. So I got my resume together and sent it over and came in for two interviews and here I am.

Well, you know my expertise is not as being an industrial seamstress. My expertise was being a college gymnastic coach. I was an assistant coach at Central Michigan for 4 years in gymnastics. So that's why I was hired. This is what Sister Carol and Sister Judy told me is why I was hired, because of that. And I had, you know, my grandmother taught me how to sew , so I sewed along the way. So I knew enough about sewing to supervise and help the ladies with preparation and just being a role model.

Currently, we are working on the two new products that "Stormy Kromer" [clothing company in Escanaba, MI] is going to put out in 2020. Two different new vests, one for men and one for women. But they entrusted us to sew out two samples based on just their sample that they sent and work out all of the little speed bumps that are in it so we have done that and it is almost ready to send back. We have been sewing vests for Stormy Kromer for 5 years. Every one that we sew, our logo is on it. And Stormy

Kromer is sold all over the world.

We are also working on some pocket squares that, like you saw at the Octoberfest, over here, Miss Jessy and Miss Marty are working on that. This is for a company called "Nosofa Club" and the founder is Christina Liedtke and I met her when I went to the Isaac Convention back in May. She was just sitting at my table so it was just a random meeting and then she contacted us and we sew these pretty scarves for her that are printed with um, such as the Detroit skyline or a New York taxi cab Yeah, they are really cool. These long scarves that you can wear as a head wrap or a scarf, tie, there are 10 different ways you can wear it. We sew them and then she sells them.

Renee is working on the bears for Grand Blanc Chamber of Commerce, which is the Teddy Bear Patrol. We have 500 scrunchies made out of seconds, mostly donated fabric or scrap from things that we work on. Deb is working on the raincoats from the Flint Fit over here. We are making one in every size and those will be in the pop-up shop in the Dryden Building downtown Flint. The raincoats are made out of material that started out being plastic water bottles. They take plastic water bottles, shred it all up, make it into pellets and then the pellets are strung out into thread. And then it is sent to a different textile mill in the Carolinas and they make this fabric that is actually 85% recycled water bottles. We make raincoats, we make tote bags out of the material. The tote bags are made out of it, which have been very successful so we will continue on with that. We have some messenger bags out of it and some purses. Water bottles made into waterproof fabric. That's my little saying "beauty out of chaos". Just like the lotus rising from the mud, such as Flint, you know, there are a lot of parallels there.

Another project we are going to work on, it's called a toque. This is another little product we have been working on the side, I mean, who doesn't need a warm hat in the winter? Right? And we have so much fleece donated so we are going to make them, embroider them with our logo on it, possibly ones that say "Flint" and we will have those down at the popup shop as well.

Yes, we have all of the children's dresses. We might hold off and put those down there at springtime. They are kind of a spring wear. We make those with donated fabric. We have the lamb and that we introduced back in the spring and that will be another item we will roll out in the spring again. We are doing the teddy bears, one of our holiday, Christmas items. Well my new thing is I am going to take them up to the hospitals, I mean to give to gift shops. So, who doesn't want to buy a little stuffed animal for the child in the hospital?

I love it here. I dream big too. I can see this much bigger than what it is, you know, with the sewing industry coming back and people supporting " Made in the USA" products, even though it is a little bit pricier. You know, that is where the trend is going to support American jobs. So, I don't see any reason why we can't be that. A marketing expert would help. Someone who really specializes in that. Reaching out, you know, it all costs money. A company that came in and filmed our sewing was a company called "Shopify" and they are actually a platform for how to boost your online sales. So maybe I will learn something through that and get some people who might be interested in helping no- profits, you know.

I could see this as being an actual business for profit. It can happen, with more marketing and connections to people who are looking for contract sewing and are willing to pay a higher wage for that product versus sending it out of the country. It's an upward struggle to get there. To be a profit company where the idea is that you ladies are really working for a company, you know, and not a social enterprise. It could be a launching pad to another career. Oh, yes, that would be lovely.

We have had ladies go to work elsewhere. Rebecca Arnell, is [now] a sewing supervisor, manufacturing supervisor at Peckham.

She said she will soon to be manufacturing coordinator. She's doing real well.

So yeah, everybody [in sewing] fills out a sheet at what they do, how many they do, how long it took them and the date. From that we can come up with this report of how long that tasks take. So, it's more time studies and also personal studies on how things are going. Everybody is accountable. It's coaching to bring out their best.

Vincente Vigil

I came here to Michigan, you know, really when I was younger, I used to come here and work in the fields as a migrant worker with my parents. I dropped out of high school in Texas when my mother got sick, to help her. When I got married and had kids I moved to Michigan to give them a better life. I've been married 37 years and have 5 kids. I told them go to school, you know, and do side jobs to give you what I didn't have, you know and graduate. And they all did. I went back to school and got my diploma too.

I knew Sister Carol, you know, from our church St Charles and Helena in Clio. I was looking for work, that was about 15 years ago. So I came over here at St Luke's Church. I cut the whole yard around the building stuff, you know and here too. And when St Luke's Church was closed they hired me here . I was hired here to assist Sister Carol, you know, to work at the Center here. I started at the north end of the building, where the Literacy Center is now, remodeling that totally so it could be the Literacy Center. I tore out the floors, the carpet, and then the, as far as the hallway goes, we had a couple of, quite a few sisters that came here and helped paint the hallway.

If maintenance work needs to be done, I'm the one. I rebuild them or fix it. {There's] a lot to be done. If I can't do it, I call somebody else to take care of it. On Tuesday and Thursday we have tables outside, it has food and sometimes clothes or, other things. And people can just come from anywhere and if they need it, they just take it. The Center has a list of people that need furniture. And when somebody donates furniture, I go get the furniture. Once you tell the sisters or somebody else, that the furniture is here, then that person calls the one who needs it and we deliver it to them

I'm here from 7 in the morning 5 days a week. The sisters do a lot for everybody, really. And that's why, they're going to be good for everybody and I'm here for them. The other people here, that work here, they're great people. I get along with everybody around here, you know? And then like I tell everybody, if anybody has a problem with whatever, come and talk to me. We can talk it out or whatever, we're all family here. And it's just a wonderful place to be. People come here because they need help and that's what we're here for, to help them. Right. And nobody's rude to them here.

And you got to feel proud about all the people that have gone through the programs here too. Then it seems like family, doesn't it, for sure. That's why I try to work with everybody. You know, everybody comes out of a program or whatever. I tried to work with them too. So that way you know, they can learn. Cause after all, the way I look at it, they come here to learn from everybody here. And when they leave here they want to find a job somewhere. You got to teach them right to get it.

Manhattan College

We're from Manhattan college which is in the Bronx. There are 8 students and then one kind of chaperone, she's a grad student. We're in Flint for a week as a kind of service immersion. We're staying at the Firestone Center and Steve Wolbert had us come here. Tomorrow we're going to North Bridge Academy. Students from Canisius College in Buffalo, New York are coming here.

We all have different reasons for coming to Flint. Um, I just wanted to learn more kind of, particularly about the water crisis and like what's being done, what has been done and what kind of caused it. Cause I was kind of like unaware of what really happened. So I wanted to come and kind of learn firsthand from the people affected.

I found out that there's more, it's, there's more issues than the water crisis issue. I wasn't, I was pretty ignorant on that. Um, yeah, I, we went to the Broome Empowerment Village yesterday and so I was very inspired by Coach Lynn now. She runs the program there. She was inspiring the children to dream big, the children of Flint. So I felt that a lot was being done in this community, by people from Flint.

We were at Habitat for Humanity. We were at the Flint Development Center where they're working on new labs. We've had a tour of the Center and met some of the people here. We're helping put the books together for orientation of the men's and women's programs which start tomorrow. 16 weeks of classes and volunteer hours. They're empowering people to overcome inner issues as well as external issues. Kind of a holistic approach which is, I think, is very beautiful.

Pat O'Callaghan

Sister Carol came up to me after Mass at St Luke's and asked me to be involved [in the Center]. That was well over 15 years ago. There were a couple of people from St. Luke's. Another early member was Chris Pierce. We were meeting at my office and restaurants and things like that. And then that morphed into a board of about 10, mostly retired folks from the church. And many of them are still on the Oktoberfest committee, very dedicated individuals. The first several years when we were the board, I would say that we were mostly a sounding board for the sisters because, you know, they did everything and we were primarily there to help them with Octoberfest. And then we turned into a business board everything improved a hundred percent. I don't know if we'd ever be to get the types of grants that we're currently able to get if we had that old board in place, and that's nothing against the old board, it's just that wasn't our skillset.

[An idea came] from one of my Rotary functions we have a reverse raffle where, you know, you had a ticket and the last one that wasn't called wins. I forget how much the grand prize was, but we were sort of stuck at [raising] $15 to 20,000 or thereabouts. We had [Octoberfest] at Dom Polski's, for several years. Then we went to St. John Vianney. We tried to cook the steak so that people would smell them coming out of the church. Probably four or five years ago we decided to go to Powers [Catholic High School] and that, frankly, I think, that was the best of what we've done in a long time. It could be the SIPI relationship or frankly, when the board turned into more of a business board that Octoberfest mushroomed into something that I never would have believed [possible]. I never believed we would be able to make $100,000

I also interviewed various employees for the Center. But for the day-to-day operation I, very frankly, did very little. One thing I was involved in was a request for a grant from the Community Foundation and we got the money for the freezer··· about $20,000 for that.

I think our current board is tremendous. I'm still quite concerned about the sisters burning themselves out. We have to make sure we have an adequate transition plan. But I'm pretty comfortable with them wherever we're going. Bob Nelson was a tremendous hire. He's a very conscientious guy. And SIPI is a great vendor to get involved. Those are the folks that I'm really comfortable with and that we're going to be around for several years.

The sisters are wonderful with networking and unfortunately haven't been able to do that much this year. But when they get out and tell their story it's the type of story that people pay attention to. I know that after the sisters spoke at my Rotary Club, there's been a couple of members that have been doing annual gifts. When this COVID stuff has done, I certainly would hope that we could get the sisters and maybe some others involved in doing those [service club] meetings and more. I think that's an area that perhaps we can explore it a little bit better. I'm really happy that Bob's there, so we can free up the sisters to do that type of stuff. And I think that's one of the emphasis that we try to do on our retreat, you know, that type of a thing. But the COVID has really kicked it our butt.

The Center is also a safe zone. Folks that are not even part of our program know that it's there. When they're in trouble, they know that's the resource. I think that's exceedingly valuable.

Joe Parks

We get a lot of schools. We get Purdue University comes every year. University of Minnesota and University of Wisconsin students come every year. So this [today] is Lansing Catholic Central. Yeah. 63 people, probably 55 kids from school. It is part of their requirements or something at school. Every kid has to have 30 hours, all the, all the Catholic schools for sure have to have 30 hours of community service to graduate every year.

An African American student from Catholic Central came up to me. He was wearing shoes that looked like Air Jordans—500 bucks. Well dressed. Probably from a family with money. And he says, "I'm embarrassed or ashamed to say that I'm a black man. I did not know that my people were living in such poverty. I would like to come back here more if that's all right." I said, you can come back here every day.

I sent an email to their administrator and let them know how much help they all were. Cause we usually stop [distributing food] at a hundred families because we just don't have the employees. Right. And with these kids, we just kept going. She just says, I love Sister Judy, here's the rules. Stop at a hundred. Then she'll go, Okay. 110. I'll go 120? Okay. Well these people don't have any food. All right. See what you can find for them. Yeah. So some of these kids from Lansing Catholic Central came in waves of 20 at a time, but they were here all day. So 150 families came and that extra 50, it wasn't all. No, I would say that's an extra 200 people got food for Thanksgiving and we managed to an empty the shelves. There wasn't any canned goods. Nothing. Wow. Nothing. We were down to absolutely nothing. And I finally had to tell Sister Judy, "We're out."

Gerry Winfrey-Carter

I am the Fifth Ward City Council person for the City of Flint. I am also the Associate Director of the literacy program here at the N.E.W. Life Center. The literacy program is sponsored by the Adrian Dominican Sisters. [How did I become part of it?] It was all God, seriously. It was all God. I saw the ad in the newspaper for an adult literacy director. And I was like "oh my God" you know I have my educational specialist degree in adult education. And I love working with adults. The teaching and learning of adults, that's my specialty.

The day I came over for the interview, I really, really fell in love with the place, I did. Um, it was, it was just so spirit filled. That's how I put it. It was so spirit filled I knew that I was supposed to be here, the day I had the interview. I knew I was supposed to be here and, um, and true enough, Sister Carol called me, maybe a couple of days later to come in for the second part of the interview process and I came in and I was able to actually observe the literacy program; observe the tutors and, you know even sit and talk to some of the adult learners and I just knew, I knew it was my job. I knew it was my job and God told me so.

I started here, I remember the day, March 8 of 2017 and I absolutely love it here. I just really love the job that I do here. I love working with the adult learners and motivating them and you know, just encouraging them and letting them know, "Look you can do this, you can do all things through Christ" which strengthens you. So, I give them the scripture, all of the time. Hey look "Don't come in here with your excuses." I don't listen to excuses. I don't.

Well, we provide adult basic education and GED prep. We pay for everything. We pay for all of your learning materials, we pay for your GED practice test, we pay for your actual GED test, for the four subjects.

Here in Flint we have a very, very large population of individuals who do not have a high school diploma or GED and so, you know, my job really, and I always ask God to use me as a vessel, and my job, my commitment to the City of Flint is to make sure we get these individuals armed with their GEDs so that they can be better prepared to go out and be self-sufficient and make the City a better place.

Right now on hand, we have 16 tutors. All volunteers. Um, and they come in ready to love on all the adult learners, encourage them, motivate them, push them, whatever it is that we need to do. We meet the adult learners where they are. Most of the learners, they say that they come by word of mouth. You know. Other agencies send people to us, I'm sure that the Flint and Genesee Literacy Network sends learners. Michigan Works sends learners to us. The Courts, we do get a lot of learners sent to us from the Court. Yes and from some of the other programs that they have here at St Luke's we will get learners from those other programs. And we work with, you know, we kind of align what they are doing for the employability program, we align it with our literacy program so that we can meet the needs of the learner and help them achieve their goals.

The first thing we do is a placement test. Our intake process, we do a placement test and from there we kind of gauge where they are as far as their reading comprehension, um, and their vocabulary level. The reason we do that is because, with all of the subjects, you have to be able to read, so, with that we take that information and we kind of see if they are already GED ready, if they are already GED ready, we don't hold them up. I don't make them go through the whole process of going through the different levels of textbooks and different things that we have, so I go ahead and say, "Okay, you are ready to take a GED ready test in language arts" and so they will take the test. If they score 145 or over, then they are able to go and actually take the actual test in language arts. So, from there, I push them, "okay, the next test is social studies, the next test is science" and usually their last test is math

Now, it is flexible because I believe for adult learners, we have to adjust to their lives to what is going on with them and so it is flexible. We have one-on-one tutoring whereas they can come in Tuesday through Friday from 8:30 to 3:30, you know, meet with a tutor. You don't necessarily have to come every day, but try to come a couple times a week, but you know also with that, I make them set smart goals. So, when they set their smart goals, I say to them, "okay, number 1, you got have a why, why are you doing this, what is your why? And number 2, when do you want to have this completed?" So, they pretty much set the dates.

They drop out. They come back; we welcome them back with open arms. Then they come and stay for 2-3 weeks, they drop back out, then they come back.

This is a holistic place, you can get all your needs met here, your spiritual needs, your emotional needs met. I love the people that I work with, you know. When I come here, I don't even feel like, you know, how you just dread going to work. It's not even like that for me. I don't even feel like I am going to work. I am just going to hang out, you know. I am going to a happy place to hang out. That's what I feel like.

Dr. Tim Branigan

I am a pathologist. I retired three years ago. I worked initially at St. Joe's and then we transitioned over to Genesys. Well, I have always enjoyed vegetable gardening. My mom got me started when I was young. I can remember picking my grandmother's green beans, you know. I always enjoyed watching things grow, planting a seed and seeing it germinate and take off from there. It is almost miraculous at times. I just get a lot of enjoyment out of it.

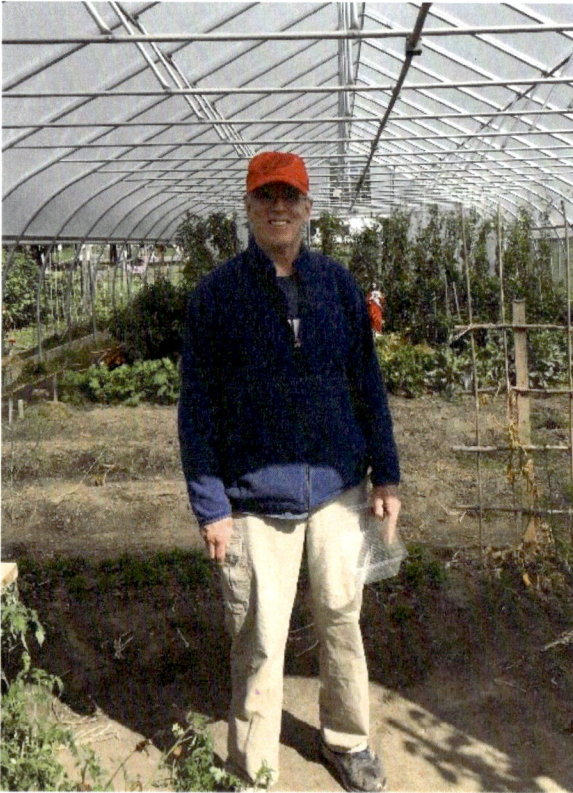

Dr. Tim Branigan

Through St. John Vianney Parish I always kind of admired what they have done here. When I was working I didn't really have a lot of time to volunteer. I remember a few times going over here on Saturdays. They used to have, I think the Food Pantry, open on Saturdays and serve a meal and I used to help out with that a little bit, but I always thought it was a good outfit and doing good things. So when I retired, I knew about the Literacy Center and I think they were asking, maybe even on the church bulletin, for tutors and teachers. I kind of have a background in science, so I have been tutoring in science [at the Literacy Center] for about 3 years.

I saw this vacant lot out here so I asked Sister Carol if she minded if I tried putting a vegetable garden in there. I said, "Do you mind if I start?" And she said, "I will hold you to it!" I am out here a lot of times on my own, but I get help from the people inside, the volunteers, some of the guys that work here on days when we are not busy, they help me do things...weed or plant or whatever. Sister Judy was the one who, I didn't think about putting a hoop house in here, but she was sort of the instigator of that. I didn't really know what I was getting into. I actually took a little course through MSU. A computer course on hoop house gardening and stuff. That was helpful.

But we still have a way to go. Our intention is to put in a sprinkler system. We have the wells. Whenever we water, we use a generator but once we get the solar system in, the intention is to put a sprinkling system in, a drip tape sprinkling system and depend on what you are growing, you put so many tapes down in a row and water would become more automatic.

Well, a lot of the produce gets handed out to either people that are coming through on Tuesdays and Thursdays with the Food Pantry or they will stop by. They are always looking for green tomatoes or whatever greens. I just gave away some green beans, cauliflower and now the ripe tomatoes The cilantro and peppers we sell. The Center sells them to Vehicle City Tacos. So, we make a little bit of profit out of it. And also the people that volunteer and work, you know, especially when squash are abundant, I drag them inside and they get taken. And outside we have perennial things, strawberry rows, I have a raspberry patch around the corner, a lot of yellow squash, something called ground cherries. Sister Judy or Sister Carol was going to try making jam out of it. It is all qualified as organic too.

Well, I do a class. I have a 5 or 6 session course, each of them are about 40 minutes. It is on vegetable gardening and I have done it for the past two years. I thought about starting a community garden. My intention that there are people that come out here and volunteer and they go "what can I plant?" and I go, "well, what do you have?" "All I have is a patio, I don't have a plot". So I was thinking, maybe we could even divide this into maybe 3 or 4 plots, 10x10. And have people work it. Maybe section off an area over here. I will talk to Sister Judy. It always feels so good here.

Rendell T.

I just want to get my GED. If you want to go to college, uh, of course you didn't get into college without a high school diploma. Right. So I needed one so this will be my first stop to go where I'm trying to go. I plan to go either to Baker or Mott Community College cause I have a book, I have a couple books I want to write. It's really based on my life and things that I been through. Like the last thing I've been through, like as you can hear my voice and see my face. So I just want to tell my story. So it will reach somebody that don't go down the same path that I did.

I was driving here in Flint. This person [who came up to my car] was on some drugs. He actually was a person I knew, a friend, almost like a brother, that's how close we was. Another person was in the vehicle I was driving. Everything happened so fast. He walked up to the car and my window was already down, but I was talking to the person in the passenger side. He pulled his gun. By the time I turned around, my first reaction was to move. So when he shot, he shot the person next to me. And when the bullet hit him he died instantly. He fell over on me so I couldn't put my car in drive to pull on.

And he actually shot again and the bullet went through my ear. Busted my eardrum so I can't hear on that side. And they had to stop the bleeding from my brain. They went in, I think though my nose, stopped to bleeding to my brain. I spent about 53 days in the hospital and I had a memory loss cause I didn't even remember my kid's name. Like I remember I just had the names mixed up. I knew one child name, I just had their names mixed up. So I came a long, a very long way. I had to learn how to walk. I had to learn how to talk as much as I'm talking now. And by the time I got out the hospital I really wanted to find him and ask, I mean, why? But by the time I'd got out of the hospital someone had killed him. A similar thing as he did to me. So like to this day it's a lot of things I don't know.

It's shut the nerve down on my left side. And the bullet fragments causes, um, uh, seizures sometimes. So I have, I was diagnosed with epilepsy. So like, uh, the first couple of years I would have 10 to 12 seizures a month. And they gave me my medicines over the years it slowed down a lot. So now I think my last one was in August. But the thing about my seizures, like I see things where I got enough time to say, " Hey, I'm about to have a seizure." I just get up, lay on my mat. So I have enough time to tell you this is what you do, this is what you don't do. Just leave me alone and let it go. Just make sure I'm not around nothing that I can hurt myself. And don't never put nothing down my mouth,

This is the third time I've been shot. I've been shot three different times, but the last time was the most severe. So the first I kinda like brushed it off because I healed so quick. I was young, and excuse my language, I was still on bullshit. So from the first time, the second time and the third time it's what made me think God telling me either you slow down or I'm gonna call you.

I just want to write a book, but I want it to go backwards. I want my book to go backwards, like the last time I was shot and then the second time to set it from the first time. The first time, like it was a chest shot and it went in and went straight out. And they put one in my lungs, but then it didn't stop me. And the second time I was shot multiple times in the foot, the ankle, the hip and the thigh.

And the third time is the time where somebody was with me and they got killed. They got killed because they were with me. And that made me feel some way because this guy wouldn't have lost his life. Maybe he would've lost his life somewhere else but not there and then.

I'm thinking of Baker so I can focus more on what I'm trying to do. I basically want them to show me, I want a class, just show me how to write a book. For like 30 years I've written things down on my own and written things down on paper, but I don't know how to properly write a book. Like from the beginning to the end, that's what I'm going to go to Baker for.

I dropped out of school soon as I got to high school. I dropped out of school. Because I wanted it to be, I wanted to be grown. Yeah. I was like, I thought I was confined and locked down. Being at home my mother was, she was on drugs and my grandmother, by the time I started living with my grandma, she really couldn't control my thinking. Not just my thinking, she couldn't control what I was, what I had already planned to do. So once I got, once I got to high school I felt I was grown. So when she got to high school, yeah, most high school, I'm following you. I told my grandma, I said, well, Hey, I'm fitting to move out because I wanted to basically, I want to see what the streets is like. I never had, like my father was around, but he never taught me how you don't do this. And I never was taught that. So everything that I know, I learned it the hard way and I lived through it.

That's what blows my mind because I did get through so much things and I live through it. I've only been in prison once. Everything that I've done, I should still be in prison. I just want to show some kid... I don't like kids getting killed. Things that I used to do, like years ago, I got one son that's in prison doing six years. I feel like it's kinda too late to talk to him. I feel like it's never too late for a child that's in middle school or in elementary. See that's all I want is one person. Get somebody onto this story and I feel like I accomplished something.

I save somebody. Right. If not, if not a thousand people, I save one person. It meant something to me and I want to tell it to somebody else. Hey, if you go down this path this is likely to happen and this will happen. If you got on this [other] path, you have a better chance of living a healthy life. Coming to the Center, it's a better path. I feel like it's a better path because it gives you another chance and another opportunity. If you don't have a GED or high school diploma, come here, get your GED and then you can move forward.

Amy Hovey

I had visited the Center when I worked for Congressman Dan Kildee. We toured the facility. Steve Wolbert asked me to meet with the sister's about fund development to be a sounding board for their pitch. I'm always very candid with my feedback so I gave them some thoughts on their pitch.

There were some vacancies on the Board of Directors, and I was asked to join. I decided to commit to be on the Board because of how genuine the Center was. I wanted to help the community, especially the North Flint Community, an area that has some additional needs compared to some of the other sections of Flint. I have been on the board for 5 years now.

"We're just here to do what we can do to make a difference in the community", whether that was clothes or food, or certainly the job training programs and the Literacy Center. The sisters' tireless effort to wanting to make a difference is so inspiring. So even, just selfishly, when you go through the doors of Saint Luke's while you're giving of your time and your expertise in nonprofit management or maybe even just what's happening in the community as a whole, you get more than you actually give every time just in that feeling of inspiration and keeping you grounded and keeping you wanting to give more back to Flint.

People feel that comfort when they walk in...the people who are there to serve as well as the people who are there to get the help.

St. Luke N.E.W. Life Center needs to tell the story of its impact in the community. The Center needs to also ensure it is being impactful, meaning not just helping one person but helping so many people. The Center doesn't want to be doing the same thing somebody else is doing. It's really hard on funders to be able to say, why are we funding two different organizations doing the same thing? For example, the Urban Renaissance Center also does lawn and landscaping business with their men similar to the Center. The two organizations are a half a mile apart. They outbid each other, And with low bids neither make any money. They are starting to work together to make each other's programs stronger by working together.

There are a lot of workforce development organizations out there and some do a better job than others. The Center doesn't prepare that many people annually who find employment so it needs to show that it helps people who are harder to employ. The Center provides the wraparound services they need to be supported during the time that they're having a job. Once they are placed, the Center still provides those supportive service for many months or whatever they need afterward. Job retention should also be tracked as that is an important part of the story. Not how many we placed, but how well we've done.

That's the kind of story that the Center needs to tell; while there are other people that do what the Center does, they don't do it in the same way. And not with the same population. So the Center is not really, in a sense, competing with the other workforce development organizations because they have a different type of clientele. And it's not even so much the abilities. It's just the poverty and the amount of crisis the population is experiencing.. They have all these different things coming at them at the same time. So the Center helps them through those obstacles. The Center has to tell that story to differentiate themselves, but also explain to funders why they might need more money that per person we put through than an average workforce development program.

The Center turns around families and helps break the cycle of poverty. Most workforce communities are development organizations just do work force development. They teach somebody a skill or the skill of being able to hold down a job. The Center is also are a food bank. They also are a soup kitchen and a clothing bank. The organization also is a Literacy Center. One day a week they have an optometrist available. They have a lawyer come in. Counseling services. Social work. They have a sewing business, a social enterprise. The Center does a lot.

I think it also puts the Center at risk sometimes. I'm not suggesting they stop doing any of those things. I just think that they always have to realize that they have some programs that are weaker and some that are stronger, and sometimes those stronger ones may have to be supportive of the weaker ones financially. We need to be cautious as a Board to make sure that we're not spreading ourselves too thin. There is a potential of losing the core programs by not paying attention to them by worrying more about new things or expanding. We have to be mindful about what we do

Bob Nelson

My first exposure to the St. Luke N.E.W. Life Center was about 7 years ago when I was a part of a neighborhood event that started and ended at St. Luke. Since then I have learned more and more about the Center, the Sisters and was always intrigued to hear about the programming and was able to become part of the team that supported the organization in 2018. SIPI, (Social Impact Philanthropy and Investment), INC. has provided various areas of support for the St. Luke N.E.W. Life Center for nearly 5 years including special event planning, program development, grant writing and finance. This support has been integral to the continued success and growth of St. Luke. As part of their team, I was able to become more familiar with St. Luke and began to understand the love, support and kindness offered to each person that received food, employment training or simply a kind word and prayer.

As part of my role at S.I.P.I, I worked with the Sisters assisting with payroll and social enterprise development. We were part of the annual fundraiser, Octoberfest, working with dozens of dedicated volunteers and staff to ensure that the event was memorable and successful. As time passed, I was more and more excited to be a part of the organization, eventually be added to the staff as the Director of Operations, a role I started in December of 2019.

It is a new role designed to support and enable Sr. Carol and Sr. Judy to deliver their gifts to the community and clients in North Flint. My role is to oversee the daily operations, provide administrative assistance and training to the staff, supervise the social enterprises, and clear the path for the Sisters to deliver the vision and mission of the St. Luke N.E.W. Life Center to those in need of it the most.

As the organization continues to grow, there are still challenges, most recently, the Covid-19 pandemic. The Sisters were even more committed to serving the community and find creative ways to ensure that everyone that needed help would receive it. We implemented a strategy to ensure our neighbors in need were still receiving food by distributing every Friday in our parking. This effort has been led by a group of very committed volunteers coming from as far as Dexter, MI to lend a hand and provide support in many other administrative areas. Our social enterprises also had to adjust and grow with the crisis as did our employment preparation class.

The traditional format of our Employment Preparation Class is 16 weeks and a temporary employment placement at the Center after graduating. During the pandemic, this format needed to be flexible to engage as many participants as possible, while also keeping everyone safe. To accomplish this, we went to a digital format for classes and were able to enroll and move forward several participants. This shift also created a new system of learning for participants, allowing them to embrace technology and learn how to use their cell phones and online meeting platforms.

Our social enterprises faced a temporary slow down when the pandemic first hit, but with a strong commitment by a few of our employees, we were able to make some incredible transitions. The sewing social enterprises flipped direction, almost overnight, to making non-medical grade face masks. We started taking orders for local businesses and received support to make masks to be handed out to the community at-large. The results are that over 16,000 masks have been made since the pandemic started!!!

Our pallet business was able to be reset with a new supervisor and returning staff members that have been able to kick things into high gear, producing several hundred pallets each week. The pallet social enterprise started in the basement of the Center with the assistance of a family-owned manufacturing company based in Howell, MI and has since grown into a shared warehouse space within the City of Flint.

The lawn care social enterprise had a successful year, gaining new clients and maintaining vacant lots around North Flint, most of them were located within 3 to 4 blocks of the Center. The members of the lawn care team learned how to use all the equipment we have available and even had some great interactions with many residents.

While the pandemic created many challenges, it also brought with it many great things. We were able to embrace and expand our use of technology to connect with many supporters of the Center through phone calls, virtual meetings, and "visits".

Overall, it has been an incredible experience that I am extraordinarily grateful for. It has been amazing to witness the kindness, love and generosity that is provided to our residents and neighbors by Sr. Carol, Sr. Judy, the staff, volunteers and everyone involved with the St. Luke N.E.W. Life Center. The best part for me is that I can get to experience it first-hand.

Jeffery Rowe

I've been involved with the Center since probably around 2000. It was kind of a gradual thing. Annette started volunteering there. And then Pat [O'Callaghan] said he was needing people to cook for Octoberfest. I said, well, I'll help. And so I think it was probably around 2008, 2009, I showed up for Octoberfest. That was a much looser event than it is now. I just showed up there and helped out. And that was my beginning with St Luke's.

We were at St. John Vianney, I think, for two or three years with me helping cook. Then I got involved with the St. Luke's board, which at that time was basically the Oktoberfest board. And then things started to evolve. Steve Wolbert working at Diplomat got the Hagermans involved and that's when I started getting more involved with board like activities there. That's how I ended up on the board and then eventually as the President. So it was, you know, one of those things, but it was all about, you know, volunteering, helping the guys.

They had just started the gentleman's classes and stuff like that. So I was there helping them with interviewing and doing their resumes and that kind of stuff. But then it became apparent through my involvement and feedback from people like Steve and other members on the board that we really needed to get the sisters help. It's been my priority as it has been for a lot of people, even back in the days of the Oktoberfest board, of really trying to help the sisters out to take a lot of the burden of the day-to-day operational and planning and that type of thing off of their plate so they could do what they do best, which is basically help train normative men and women and help fundraise for St. Lukes.

One of the things that I am most proud of is that we've really seen a maturation process at St. Luke's, both in the programs that we offer and in our volunteers and staff and particularly in our board too. It's really helped St. Luke's message and mission to the point now where we really are a pretty rock-solid organization that we can build off and go forward. The sisters are much more comfortable than they were. It wasn't without taking some convincing and some fits and starts, but they both realize now that this is a good thing. The Center can flourish and grow and prosper.

We've had our growing pains. Things like the Stormy Kromer thing were kind of like a gift out of nowhere. We started it and, it just took some time to get it there. But, you know, now that's pretty much a business. You're going to have ebbs and flows but we've been able to really build a solid core both in that sewing program and the lawn care program. And now the pallets, which has been one of those things I think is just an amazing. We've tried some other things. We really tried like heck to get that baking program off the ground. It's like most things. You gotta have the right person there to run it. And I don't think we've had that. We had a lot smarter. We know that it's gotta be done right and have the right people in place for that to work. So we've gotten smarter over the business development department. Sometimes it's good to say, no,

I'm very proud of all the programs that have come through and they just built upon like the literacy program, which is fantastic. And, you know, it's, well-funded. We're getting better equipment. We get grants for it. Now St. Luke's has the reputation that they do. They're just an absolute, essentially needed service in the North End of Flint. And people recognize that. Everybody from the large donors and grantors, the Motts and et cetera. They're people know who St Luke's is. And they know what great, hardworking, dedicated people the sisters are. And they know if they give us some money it's going to be spent wisely and well.

The basic blocking and tackling is being done now. The tax forms are being done on time. Our bookkeeping is rock solid. Bills are getting paid on time and checks are getting deposited quickly. It's from the early days at the we've, you know, we've really matured quite nicely from the early days.

It's been kind of interesting and we talked about this at the last board meeting. The Covid has actually been probably a blessing in disguise for St. Luke's. Not having to pay for the food pantry is taking a huge expense off our books. It's made us rethink some things, like look at what happened with Oktoberfest. It looks like Oktoberfest is going to be every bit of the success that was the previous year. Maybe we've changed our model somewhat on that. Who knows? Going forward there's always a long list of things that need to be accomplished. [We need to be] always continually improving our policies and our procedures and paying attention to our strategic plan. It is very, very important. The needs in the North End of Flint are not going to go away anytime soon.

I had a chance to hear Father Greg Boyle who founded Homeboy Industries this last winter down in Florida. It was very, very interesting. He works with inner city gangs in Los Angeles. They kinda just started doing certain things, baking and stuff like that. And then they went into education. So it kind of evolved for them just about the same way it did for St. Luke's. Of course being in inner city Los Angeles it's a bit bigger and larger operation. But [like Father Boyle] we've got the base that we can build a future on for St. Luke's and keep it strong, keep it relevant and really make a difference in educating men and women in the North End. And that's really what it's all about. The other services are nice, but the biggest thing that's going to make a change is us getting those men and women the education, the training and the jobs that they need. And then those seeds just keep growing and sprouting and multiplying,

You can never underestimate getting that confidence that you need to go out and do something like getting a job. Cause it's scary if you've never had to hold a job. If they've been rejected so many times because of their past or something like that, us being able to change that for them and giving them the confidence and giving them the chance is priceless. We may see some of it, but you know, most of this hopefully happens afterwards. If some of our graduates are doing well, hopefully their families, their kids will be the first one to go to college. Something. like would be absolutely fantastic. As we're watching this evolve, there may be something we can do like starting some sort of St. Luke's scholarship program for graduates and kids if they're going to go to college, which would be great.

There's just amazing stories out there. And many of us just cannot fathom what they've been through, what they've been exposed to. You know, we think sometimes we've had some hardships in our life, but we've never had anything like that. I never had anybody shoot at me. All you have to do is come into St Luke's and spend a day and you get it. You know. You're changed. You understand the need, um, your cynicism kind of melts away. You see how the sisters put it out there and have dedicated their lives to helping people and giving their all for them. And you just want to do more for people, you know, that becomes the overriding thing. And I've said this to a couple of people. I said if there was anybody that I ever thought should be sainted, like Mother Teresa is a saint, and the same thing for Sister Carol and Sister Judy.

Sister Carol

We thank God every day for entrusting us with the St. Luke N.E.W. Life Center. The tireless volunteers who have done so much, the wonderful employees who do more than their jobs require and the grateful recipients whose lives have been enriched by being part of NEW Life have all contributed to create an oasis of safety and peace and love in the north end of Flint. And without our generous donors and foundations, none of this would be possible. We have grown to be a well-functioning charitable organization which takes in structurally unemployable women and men, trains, educates and conditions them to be able to work, then gives them a job and eventually finds outside employment for them all to better their lives, their families lives and the Flint community.

Once we can reopen our doors there is so much more to be done. We fear there has been an increase in domestic violence which has not been reported because of COVID-19. More counselling for men as well as women is needed. Jobs have been lost so a greater need exists for food and clothing and other support. And we look forward to being able to take our mission to the surrounding areas. Ironically we should also return to our street ministry. So many people in need cannot travel to NEW Life. We already deliver food to 17 families in the neighborhood because they have no way to get to the Center. And now because of the virus our storage space is full of clothing, household goods and other donations. We have had to stop taking donations. So when we are able to do so, we would like to go directly to those in need who cannot come to us. But that is going to be a whole new program.

We could not hold our Octoberfest fundraiser where over 300 people come to Powers Catholic High School on a Sunday and enjoy a steak or chicken dinner. After dinner we would have presentations about the Center and auctions and other fundraisers. In 2020 we started a home dinner program. In exchange for a contribution to the Center, people would have a dinner for family and friends, usually 10 people, in their home. The Center would provide the steaks, chicken and all the fixin's ready to cook and serve. After dinner a zoom meeting would let us explain the work of the Center and allow the guests to hear the story of one of the ladies who had sought our help.

For some time, now, we have thought about a baking program. Some of our women do not have the skills to learn to sew. We need to find them some other employment. Many of them have expressed a love of baking or an interest in learning to bake. We need that special person with baking skills and the time and ability to run the program for us. Then we need the space, the equipment and the funding to get it going.

But most of all we need personal contact with everyone involved with NEW Life and everyone who wants to be involved with NEW Life. The caring looks, the kind words and the hugs give so much comfort to the troubled. Thank you for "listening" to the Voices of N.E.W. Life and pray that we can get together soon. God Bless.

Sister Judy

When one of us is presented with something new to add to our mission, we turn to the other and say, "Can we do that?" Then if at all possible we start in. And we work with every other agency or entity we can to carry it out. We especially value our work with the YWCA on domestic violence. But their shelters for abused women and children have been continuously full since they started. There is a great need to open more shelters. We have also learned in our work with battered women that if we could change the lives of the men responsible for the abuse, we would better the lives of everyone. But that too takes a lot.

When Dr. Tim asked if he could start a plot of fruits and vegetables on our land, we said we would hold him to it. Now look at our hoop house where we grow not only fruits and vegetables to give to the needy (and even sell some), but we grow flowers as well. I would like to start a second hoop house and grow flowers to sell thereby making Flint a nicer and more beautiful place. Perhaps, too, the land around the hoop house could be divided in allotments. Dr. Tim and others could teach some neighbors how to manage a garden.

We realized early on that the path of our mission has no end. We also learned that there is no limit to how wide it can grow. We are so thankful and grateful to all those who have helped along the way and who continue to do so. If the "Voices" of N.E.W. Life have spoken to you, we invite you to help in whatever way you think best. God Bless.

APPENDIX

Colleges who have sent volunteers to St Luke N.E.W. Life Center

Auburn

Canisius College

Georgia Southern

Harris Stowe

Lake Superior State

Loyola University

Manhattan College

Marquette

Michigan State University

New Mexico State

Parkland College

Purdue

Siena Heights

Spelman

St. Louis University

St. Martin's - Seattle

St. Mary's University of Minnesota

University of Michigan

University of Wisconsin - Madison

Virginia Tech

Churches outside Genesee County
who have recently hosted Mission Appeals

St Mary Student Parish, Ann Arbor.

St. Mary Church, Charlotte, MI

St. Joseph Church, St. John's, MI

St. Andrew Church, Saline, MI

St. Martha Church, Okemos, MI

Cristo Rey Church, Lansing, MI

St. Francis of Assisi Church, Saginaw, MI

Resurrection of the Lord Church, Saginaw, MI

St. John Student Center/

St. Thomas Aquinas Church, East Lansing, MI

SS Peter & Paul Church, Ruth, MI

St. Mary Church, Parisville, MI

St. Isadore Church, Palms, MI

St. Joseph Church, Dexter, MI

Foundations and Organizations who have issued grants to St Luke N.E.W. Life Center

Charles Stewart Mott Foundation

Ruth Mott Foundation

Dominican Adrian Sisters

Congregation of the Sisters of St. Joseph

AG Bishop Foundation

Community Foundation of Greater Flint

Catholic Extension

Nartel Family Foundation

Conrad Hilton Fund for Sisters

Brezlaff Foundation

Consumers Energy Foundation

Dollar General Foundation

Quota International

Raskob Foundation

United Way of Flint & Genesee County

Zonta Club of Flint